Daddy's Girl

A Memoir
It's Always Been Him

MARIESA MOORE-GENTRY

ISBN 978-1-966229-02-5 (paperback)
Printed in the United States

Cover design by Mariesa Moore-Gentry

Published by Your Best Dash
www.yourbestdash.com

To my dear siblings, who have been a constant source of love throughout my life. Thank you for being my lifelong companions and for sharing with me the joys and sorrows of life. This book is dedicated to you, with all my love and gratitude for being the best siblings a person could ask for.

Contents

Foreword

Research tells us that fathers are important. No matter who you are, having a father or father-figure to lead, guide, protect and correct you can make a significant difference in your life. His presence, words and behavior can make positive impacts on his children and, as a result, are often replicated in their lives. Moreover, this is especially true between fathers and daughters.

Daughters thrive on the attention and attentiveness of their fathers. From him, she receives instruction and identity. It is through his eyes that she sees herself. It stands to reason, then, that the converse is also true. Daughters are shaped by the experiences of and sometimes the absence of their fathers. If she cannot find reassurance or stability in their relationship, she is left wanting and her decisions often reflect that void. Regardless, it is crucial to note, whether in person or absent, fathers matter.

If this imperative is true regarding natural relationships, how much more are we impacted by our spiritual connectedness (or the absence thereof) with our Heavenly Father? He is our Creator–the Author and the Finisher of our faith. Romans 8:15 reminds us that Believers are adopted into the family of God and are permitted to call Him Abba, Father (paraphrased). That means we have full rights and authority as "sons" (or daughters) of God to "come boldly before his throne" to ask of Him what we will. He, in turn, as a good Father, provides for our spiritual, emotional and physical needs.

Despite this unconditional access, it is often life's challenges and our earthly relationships that push us to a place of understanding our absolute need to fall into the arms of our loving Daddy. It is this parallel consideration of seeing oneself as a daughter through the eyes of a natural father and becoming THE daughter as purposed by our Heavenly Father that creates both necessary tension and essential growth.

In *Daddy's Girl*, Mariesa Moore-Gentry takes the reader on a journey through her life in a loving, God-centered family as she navigates becoming a young woman–detours and all. She gracefully and tenderly paints the picture of the importance of having a loving father. Moore-Gentry allows us to be a "fly-on-the-wall" during some of her family's most challenging moments. But reminiscent of the story of the prodigal son (though not as dramatic), she reminds the reader that no matter how far you stray, the arms of a loving father running to meet you during your darkest seasons makes all the difference in the world. Through every struggle faced by Moore-Gentry (I won't give them away here), it would be her father's reassurance, trust and instruction that would allow her to drive herself back to the destination that God purposed for her from the beginning.

I encourage everyone reading *Daddy's Girl* (particularly women), to reflect on your own relationship with your father. Whether present or absent, he made an indelible mark on the person you would become. Getting to the root of whatever those experiences were can be the license that gives you permission to heal and/or to thrive. Most importantly, I encourage you to reflect on your relationship with your Heavenly Father. Ever present, He will never leave you nor forsake you. He knows a thing or two about wood (you'll get that later) and the pain it can cause. He also knows how to turn trauma into triumph. In fact, through Him we can share the testimony, "Death where is your sting? Grave where is your victory?!"

Dear Reader, you will not only be blessed by *Daddy's Girl*, you will be healed and set free. I'm excited for your journey. Now buckle up and ride!

Dr. Matisa D. Wilbon – May 3, 2023, Author of "Undefeated: Prayer Never Loses."

Preface & Prayer for You

When I was around ten years old, my mother gifted me a journal. It had a cute picture of a golden retriever puppy on the front of the hardback cover. As I flipped through the blank, lined pages, I wondered what I was supposed to write in it. I'm not aware if Mom had a specific intention when she gave it to me, but I am sure that God laid it on her heart to do so.

He knew what would fill its pages, as well as the pages of journals to come, as the years went by. He knew that journaling would become therapeutic for me. He knew that it would help develop my love for writing and details, and eventually, its contents would provide content for this book.

Journaling has helped me in more ways than I could ever express and do it justice. I've always encouraged others to journal and even gave some as gifts. A student of mine brought to my memory something I told her probably 15 years ago: "Let your writing be your voice, whether it be the glue that holds you together or a safety net allowing you to fall apart." Little did I know, Mom's obedience would impact the rest of my life and the lives of those around me.

In the 11th grade, I wrote a paper, "A Detour in the Road of Life." I received an A on it, brought it home, and showed it to my parents. They both enjoyed it, and Dad asked for a copy. In it, I spoke about a situation we had just gone through and come out victorious.

Many years later, I found that paper; God laid it on my heart to use for the beginning of this book. Much life has been lived since the paper's completion, so there's definitely a story to tell. Not knowing how it would come together, I began writing.

I set the book down for several years but picked it up again to add a bit more. This pattern continued for quite some time. When I'd write, it caused me to revisit some not-so-pleasant times, caused some emotions to surface that I hadn't fully dealt with, and caused me to reflect on sights, sounds, and feelings I didn't feel ready to pen. I even wrote and published my first book while this one sat.

Toward the end of my completing that first book in 2019, God did something in me and healed my heart. I could think about the past and smile because I saw how His grace and love carried me through.

In 2021, He pressed it in my heart to pick this book up again and give it some of my attention. I told Him that I would not rush the process but allow Him to write through me. I had no timeline, no date for completion, but just trusted that His timing was perfect. With each writing session (some more difficult than others), I've felt His presence surround me to remind me that He was with and using me. I've poured my heart into these pages with thoughts of who would be encouraged by this piece of my story. With that said, I'd like to pray for you at this time:

Father God,
I come before You today, thanking You for being God. You are our provider, our peace, and our strength. There is none like You. We call you holy, holy, holy, Lord God Almighty. We bow before You with gratefulness in our hearts for who You have always been to us.

Father, I pray for the person who's reading this book. I pray that with every page turned, Your presence is made manifest in their midst. I thank You that You are in total control of what they recollect about their lives as they read this portion of mine. I thank You that as they read, they hear what You are speaking into their hearts, even if it's not written on the page. I pray that they will come to know You more and more and that their hunger for You increases.

Father, I thank You for how You have brought them through 100 percent of their good and bad days. I thank You that You will never leave or forsake them. I pray that this book would be a blessing in their lives and that they receive exactly what You have for them in its pages.

In Jesus' name,
Amen.

Disclaimer:
This book may contain potentially triggering content and sensitive issues. Reader discretion is advised.

Introduction

When I was in my late teens, I drove my mother and a lady from our church down to our church's annual assembly–it was held in a city two hours away. While traveling, we ran into an intense downpour of rain. Vehicles were parked under bridges waiting for the storm to pass. Other drivers turned on their hazard lights to communicate that they were having trouble seeing, so they were driving slower than usual. For a long period, it was difficult to see the road clearly in front of me, so I also slowed down and turned on my hazard lights. Mom checked on me to make sure I was okay, but other than that, it was quiet. The conditions of the road were not favorable; they had the potential to make me stop, so I had to divert all of my focus to driving safely to our destination.

If at any point I felt that I couldn't continue because of the severity of the storm, I would have pulled over. I didn't know how long it would last or how long we would have to travel before it ceased, so I prayed and asked God to help us travel through it.

I sat in a sanctuary filled with people once we arrived at the church. God drew my attention back to the drive. He told me that just as He took me through that physical storm, He would also take me through any and every storm that would come into my life. He didn't tell me that He would take me through *some* of them, but *all* of them. It also included the ones that I would create. At that time, I wasn't thinking along those lines, but I held onto His word.

In the pages of this memoir, I share some very intimate moments of my and some of my family's journey, navigating life's ups and downs and trying to go through each storm. I didn't always hold onto the word God gave me or put my trust in Him, but God is relentless in His pursuit. As many times as I've felt like I failed Him,

I've come to realize that His love for me is unconditional. It's a love that surpasses my mistakes and shortcomings. In fact, it's through my failures that I've come to know God's love, grace, and mercy more intimately.

You will read a candid account of how God used my failures to mold me into who I am today. It's a story of redemption, hope, and how God can turn even the most painful experiences into something beautiful. We often feel the pressure to be perfect in every aspect of our lives, but through my journey, I've learned that true beauty and strength come from embracing our imperfections and trusting in God's perfect plan for our lives.

Whether you're young and just starting on your journey or a seasoned veteran looking for renewed inspiration, I hope my story will remind you of God's unwavering love and grace for you. No matter where you are in life, no matter the mistakes you've made or the successes you've achieved, whether I'm informing or reiterating it to you, I want you to know that you are your Daddy's girl (or boy). It's my hope that the relationships you're going to read about in the pages that follow point you toward Him.

Sincerely,
Mariesa ♡

One

"Girls, Dad *does* have cancer." These five words changed my life. On the bitter winter evening of Monday, December 13, 1999, everything suddenly grew colder as the news of this potentially fatal disease plagued my family. There was an invader who was, in no way, welcomed in our family, yet there it was lurking, dwelling, poisoning, trying to claim another victim.

I was only 15 years old and had never come this close, almost face to face, with this monster. I watched a couple of television shows and movies in which characters had it. They suffered through chemotherapy. They lost their hair. Their bodies seemed to dwindle to skin and bones while they fought for their lives. The treatment that was said to make them better and kill the affliction, sent poison through their bodies and killed bad cells *and* good cells. When I heard the word cancer, I immediately associated it with the terrible symptoms I had seen: unbearable fatigue, horrific bouts of vomiting, and despite extreme efforts, ultimately leading to death. *Is this what my daddy was about to experience? Is this what our family was about to witness and endure?* The questions swirled in my head without retreat.

When I was around five or six years old, I thought about our close family relationships. I knew I had the best mommy, daddy, brother, and sister in the whole wide world. We deeply loved each other. At that same tender age, I thought about how death would one day separate us, but it was okay because we would, one day, all be in Heaven together. I remember crying; the hot tears rolled out the corner of my eyes, wetting my pillow as I lay in bed at night thinking about Mommy and Daddy not being there with me. My mind flooded with questions like, *What would I do? Who would take care of me? Who would I live with? How would I get food?*

Now, some ten or so years later from my ever so young thoughts, had the time come? I thought that this might be how our family dynamic would change. I wasn't ready for my daddy to leave. I didn't want him to suffer, nor did I want to watch him suffer. A few days before the wind was knocked out of me on that cold night, Dad mentioned to me that he had a biopsy due to some previous abnormal tests. Not realizing the severity of the situation at that moment or not wanting to deal with reality, I went about my day and didn't give it much thought.

In the same conversation that evening, Dad told me to pray. He modeled prayer my entire life. He had laser surgery to remove kidney stones during my middle school years. The morning of that surgery, he told me to pray for him. While getting ready for school, I closed the door, knelt in the bathroom with the most sincere heart, and went before God on behalf of my daddy. In that prayer, I remember specifically asking God to guide the hands of the surgeons, to allow the surgery to be a success, and for there to be no complications. While in the waiting room, I put my trust in the Lord. I knew that I prayed, and He was a prayer-answering God, so my faith was strong.

Later that day, after the surgery, Dad lay in his recovery bed, looked up at me, and said, "God answered your prayers." That moment was amazing. To be assured, to have confirmed once again that the Almighty God, Creator of Heaven and Earth heard little ole' me in that bathroom, was pivotal.

So yes, after hearing the news, I prayed when Dad told me to. I heard him and I knew without a shadow of a doubt that God answered prayers, but this felt like it was just too much. Not too much for God of course, *but* I hadn't heard of many survival stories. So, all I could do was sit there with this blank look on my face, all the while confused about the best way to react. When he called my sister and me into the living room, it was as if I already knew what would come out of his mouth, but are you ever really ready for a moment like that? When that devastating, faith-testing, consuming thing comes your way, are you ever prepared? Will you ever be ready? Don't get me wrong, I knew about faith.

The first Sunday school teacher with whom God blessed me, taught me about faith. She had all of us in class #5 individually stand on a desk in front of her. One by one, she asked us if we had faith. She told us that if we had faith, then we would believe and trust her to catch us when we jumped off the desk into her arms. Some of us were a little hesitant but others displayed their faith quickly. Each time, no matter our size or how wildly we jumped, she caught us. We believed, even though we hadn't seen her do it for us until our turn was over. Then we could look back and know we could trust her.

My first faith lesson out in the "real world," came at the age of nine. I'd just started fourth grade at a new, bigger school and I was nervous. A skosh into the school year, a classmate called himself "liking" me. He grew angry because the feeling wasn't mutual. I know I wasn't mean about it because I was too timid to be. I don't know if angry is the best word to use to describe his feelings considering what happened. It was to the point where, the next day, he brought a knife to school, showed it to me, and told me he was going to kill me. *We are nine years old, really?* I kept my eye on him and tried to keep my distance for the rest of the day. It would seem that the logical thing to do, instead of just avoiding him, would've been to tell the teacher. However, I didn't want to cause an uproar and I didn't want to be labeled as a "tattletale." God certainly protected me, and upon getting home from school, I told my parents. Instead of getting upset and stepping out of character and integrity, they prayed with me. They asked me if I had faith and if I believed that God would answer my prayers. My answer was, "Yes" because I knew exactly what that was. I remembered jumping off that desk and my Sunday school teacher catching me. God would catch me too; I just knew He would before I even saw it. At that time, I believed partially because of my parents' beliefs. When I returned to school, I learned that this young man moved and was transferred to a different school. This was a monumental moment. *God, You heard me! You answered my prayer!* With that situation, my faith began to grow. I learned that I could depend on God. At that point, I believed because I encountered Him for myself.

That night sitting there with my dad, I couldn't see beyond the massive fiery dart of cancer, but faith isn't what I see. As we sat, hurt was felt, but Dad let it be known that he was not going to go down in sackcloth and ashes (be sorrowful and start mourning). He didn't want us to either, so I attempted to mask the worry that crept in and possibly showed on my face. *What next? Where do we go from here?* Rather than worry, we would take it one day at a time. Ready or not, here we go...

Two

The good news was that the doctors caught Dad's cancer very early. Gratefulness flooded our hearts. After going to private conferences with the urologist, Dad concluded to have surgery. It was scheduled for Friday, February 18, 2000, at 8 a.m. After that, everything would be just fine and go back to normal. I thought back to how I prayed to God regarding Dad's health before, and He answered. I knew that if God brought Him through surgery and illness before, He would do it again. My faith was attached to previous encounters.

From December to February, the prayers went forth and life continued. During that time, I recall going to the flooring store one day after school with my parents. They wanted to improve the kitchen with a new, fresh coat of paint in a different color and replace the old kitchen floor with a more modern one. The walls were a yellowish-beige color. The old floor was green and yellow vinyl with a repeating old-fashioned design on it. I sat on that floor many times to play jacks, set up dominoes, or make a hideout between the stove and refrigerator. So many times I would look down and stare at that floor while staying as still as a statue to avoid being burnt by the hot comb. I walked across that floor in frustration sometimes because my knees and face were greased with the leftover TCB hair grease from my Mom's hands after she did my hair. There were a plethora of memories attached to the kitchen floor.

Eleven days before the surgery, Dad painted the kitchen a pretty baby blue color. He used the same blue to paint the walls of the landing. What we called the landing was the entryway into our house from the side door. There were three steps leading up to the side porch, a turn to the right, and then one step up into the door, and one would be on the landing.

I usually became pretty excited when Dad took on a new house project. Painting the kitchen was no different. It didn't matter that I was just shy of 16 years old, I enjoyed watching or even helping him do some things around the house. After school that day, I watched him paint the walls and the ceiling while he was on his ladder, but every day I watched him walk in faith. He continued to preach, teach, and do what God designed him to do on Earth.

Faith was exercised and home-cooked meals along with delectable desserts were delivered and enjoyed. Dad had such a loving support system that consisted of family, friends, and church family. God had us, so we would come out victorious and give Him glory because He was going to work a miracle. Soon, this would all be a distant memory.

On the morning of surgery, our family got up at 4 a.m. to prepare for a long day. Anticipation, concern, and anxiety were bottled up inside me, so there was no way that I would have been able to sit in school. This was a day of togetherness, prayer, and reflection.

My brother drove us, and we arrived at the hospital at 6 a.m. and waited. When the hospital staff took Dad to prepare him in the pre-op area, we were all surrounded by so much love—members of our family, friends, and church family were there offering support. They were in the trenches with us. They, too, were praying for their Bishop, their pastor, their relative, their friend, and his family. We truly needed them.

Right before he was taken into surgery, everyone who was there with us had the opportunity to gather around his bed. There Dad was, not dressed in his usual suit or casual clothes, but in a hospital gown and attire for surgery. As unnerving as it was, some laid hands on him, while others held hands and prayed. At the time, there was a sweet member from our church who just happened to be the nurse who would wheel him to the operating room. Dad was covered.

I cannot recollect most of what happened while he was in surgery, but I do know that time seemed to creep by. Our group of love lessened some of the stress. We were never left alone.

As time seemed to grow longer, some anxiety set in. The surgery was supposed to be a certain number of hours, but approximately an hour after the set time, he still wasn't out of surgery. We hadn't heard anything from the doctors, so members of the church started to ask the receptionist in the waiting area for an update. Soon after, my mother's hospital pager gave a fierce buzz. She moved hastily to the front desk. It was explained to her that there were complications. *Complications? What kind of complications? Please don't say that my daddy died. I prayed, so he is going to be fine, right?* They assured Mom that everything was okay, but the surgery would take an additional hour. We were comforted to hear the news because it could've gone differently. A little relief graced us, so my siblings and I decided to go and get food as the surgery was close to ending.

When we arrived back at the hospital, Dad was already put into his room. We were glad to see him open his eyes again and talk to us with a smile on his face. God did it again! I thanked Him for taking a huge piece of my heart through surgery. As he delighted us with his words, he told us to go home and get some rest, but we stayed for a while longer before leaving.

We went home and rested a little while, but we went back to the hospital that night. As he faded in and out from the anesthesia, Dad told us that he had so many visitors. Since he wasn't all the way with us, we just sat around and kept him company during the times he faded in. Other visitors came in that night and throughout his hospital stay. Every day after school, I went to sit with him until the day he came home. With each visit, it seemed he had new balloons, cards, or flowers. I was very grateful for the wonderful treatment from the nurses and everyone involved in this process. Dad would tell me on various occasions that he didn't "want for anything," and I was elated to hear that.

When I came home from school on Wednesday, February 23rd, Dad was there, home from the hospital. Flowers and cards were abundant, so our house smelled like a florist. Our home was also loaded with fruit baskets, meals, and cakes. The train of visitors continued and the road to recovery was in full swing.

As the days went by, Dad gained more strength. He walked with a bit more speed and was able to do more on his own. He even continued to take care of the church business. Since he wasn't permitted to drive for a while, I drove him around. I had my learner's permit, so I was glad for the opportunity for a few reasons.

I wanted more experience driving, I loved it, and it was something my dad looked forward to as well. We went to the bank, the mall, to eat, and wherever else he told me to take him. His schedule was so busy before his surgery and since he was to be in the house the majority of his post-op time, it was quite an adjustment for him. He would wait for me to get home from school and ask where I was taking him. In a way, I felt sorry for him because his independence was partially and temporarily gone. My mother went back to work a few days after he was discharged, so he was by himself. His countenance would light up when I walked into the house. Loving to see him light up, I looked forward to getting home and experiencing it. I guess you could say I was a Daddy's girl. No, I know for sure that I was definitely a Daddy's and a Mommy's girl.

I remember one specific day after school, I drove him to the mall. He mentioned that he wanted to buy a camera for my mom and one for my sister. As we entered the mall and walked past several stores to get to the camera shop, my dad lifted both of his hands in the air. *What is he doing?* Right there in what seemed to be the middle of the mall, he began to loudly boast from a grateful heart the goodness of the Lord. At that time, I glanced around in embarrassment because he was loud, but if I knew then what I know now, I would have joined in with him. Instead, I bowed in my heart and thanked God a little more quietly. All the while, he exclaimed that he made it and that God did it!

Thereafter, his strength was almost fully come. He only missed one week of church services and the following week, he went on Sunday morning. The congregation was glad to see their pastor walk down the aisle one more time. Giving all thanks to God though Dad was not out of the woods, we could see the light at the end of the tunnel.

Day by day, he progressed pretty quickly. His doctor told him that he was doing extremely well. He began to drive again after a few weeks and regained his independence. We'd finally arrived at a bit of calm during the storm.

Three

On Saturday, March 25, 2000, just 36 days after Dad's cancer surgery, his mother passed away. She suffered a heart attack just days prior. That night after Dad told me she passed, I went to the movies with friends–we saw something scary. I've never been one to engage a great deal in horror movies, but I wanted to get out of the house, especially after finding out that my grandma died. I was sad, but I was also a teenager. I didn't know what to do with my feelings, nor was I aware that I needed to do anything with them. I wanted to go have fun and not think about how I was feeling, or more importantly, how Dad or my family must have felt.

Do you know how something will happen or go wrong and you forget about it for a little while, but then you keep toiling in your mind trying to remember what was bothering you? Then you finally remember and it makes you sad all over again. Why do we do that? Throughout the movie, I recalled the fact that my grandma died.

Growing up, she lived in my dad's hometown which was about eight and a half hours away from our residence. I couldn't go to her house every day or even call her frequently. Making a long-distance phone call cost money, so we were unable to call as much as we desired. Instead, she and I wrote letters to each other. I still have some of the cards and handwritten letters she sent me.

I remember Grandma P. coming to our house to visit when I was young. I enjoyed having her live with us, even if it was just for a little while. Both of my grandmothers lived in different states, so I never experienced what it was like to have a grandparent around. There was no teaching on how to make Grandma's famous dishes, no eating her good cooking on random days or holidays, and being dropped off at her house was foreign to me. So, I was so excited to have Grandma around. During her visit, she would tell me to "shake a leg" and I would literally do it because I was too young to understand the idiom. I stayed up with her and watched baseball at night while she explained some of what was happening in the game, but I was more interested in being with her. When it came time for her to fly back home, we were able to push her in a wheelchair all the way to the stairs of the plane. We said our sad goodbyes and watched her ascend the stairs, disappointed that she had to leave.

A few years after her visit, Dad and I made the trip back to his hometown for his cousin's funeral. It was just the two of us. The ride was long, but I loved that time with him. During the course of this trip, he took me to Grandma's house. He stayed for a short time and then he left. I'd never been dropped off or left with a grandparent before and I have to admit, I was excited but felt a little like I didn't want to say or do the wrong thing. I didn't know her real well because I hadn't been around her much. What I did know is that I loved her because she was my grandma. Because of her, I had my daddy.

Grandma lived in a small, 588-square-foot house across the yard from my dad's youngest sibling and only sister's house. Upon entering, you were greeted by a small, enclosed porch with windows all around. Beyond that was the living room where family photos were displayed and memories were contained. On the wall, hung framed photos of three of my uncles and my dad. Each of them wore their military attire; one Sailor, one Airman, and two Marines. Dad was a Marine. There was a short hallway that led to the kitchen towards the back of the narrow home. On one side of the hallway was a bathroom and on the other side, was another small room–either a closet or a laundry area. The part of the house that I spent the most time in was the kitchen, at the end of the hallway. Just off of it, was her bedroom towards the left and there was another door on the far right. The refrigerator that housed her beloved Pepsi and sat under her large carton of cigarettes, was close to the door on the right. In the middle stood her kitchen table, where we sat and talked.

At that kitchen table, Grandma and I played her handheld Wheel of Fortune game made by Tiger Electronics. I liked the show, enjoyed trivia, and loved to solve puzzles. This was a good way for us to bond more. While we played, she smoked her cigarettes and drank Pepsi like it would go out of style. I wanted to say something about smoking because I knew it was bad for her health, but I also didn't feel comfortable doing so–I was a child. Every now and again, you could hear the rumble and clickety-clack, clickety-clack, clickety-clack gradually grow louder and louder as a train would fly down the railroad track in her backyard, shaking the house and blaring its horn.

She had a cat that I did not care for and was quite afraid of. I think the cat disliked me just as much. It followed me around the table as I struggled to get away from it and it brushed itself up against my leg when it passed under the table. Grandma told me that it wasn't going to bother me, but I saw the way it looked at me. Despite the presence of the cat, Grandma and I had a fine time together. We enjoyed each other's company and this was one of the fondest memories I had with her.

Frequently, while sitting in the movies, I was able to cast my mind back to what was bothering me. Grandma died, she was gone. I had as much fun as I could while there, but the thought of her death was still with me.

After the movies, I got back home fairly late. We had church in the morning, so I did my best to come in quietly to not disturb my parents. I thought they may have been sleeping. The extremity of my daddy's grief was something that I could not fathom because I didn't know what it was like to lose a mother. I wasn't exactly sure how to be there for my dad. Before I left for the movies earlier that evening, I remember the sad look on his face. I knew I didn't want to see that look again upon returning. So I was as quiet as I could be, and once in bed, I was as still as a log.

I struggled to get to sleep. As I lay there, I found myself dozing off a little but also thinking of the day's events–so I couldn't rest. It was dark and quiet throughout the house; but in my mind, my thoughts were so loud. All of a sudden, I heard a loud noise pierce the silence which hovered overhead. It was indescribable. I don't know if it was possible to lie more still than I had been, but I froze. Hurt penetrated my ears as the sounds of heart-wrenching sobs escaped from my daddy's core and echoed throughout the house. I just laid there, listening to my hero wail. I didn't know what to do or how to comfort him. I couldn't imagine his pain in those moments; I could hear it, but I couldn't *truly* feel it. I hurt for him. I was scared because I'd never heard a sound quite like that before. I had seen him wipe a few tears away during worship, but this was very different. I continued to lie there, still as a board as my heart pounded within my chest. Eventually, I fell asleep. The sound of that night is one that I will probably never forget.

Several days later, we traveled to attend Grandma P.'s funeral. Some of our church family and my dad's friends accompanied us in support. As we drove, we stopped every two hours because Dad developed a blood clot in his leg after his surgery. He needed to walk to help dissolve the clot and to keep other clots from forming. With each stop, or at least most of them, I watched as he walked away from the car on the shoulder of the highway. He appeared to grow smaller in the distance as he walked down the road. As cars and semi trucks flew by, they shook our car violently. Dad was consistent in following his doctor's orders and with each stop, we got closer to our destination before eventually making it there.

Grandma's wake was the evening we arrived and her funeral was the next day. At the funeral home, I looked down at Grandma laying in her casket, wearing one of her housecoats or as some would call it, a moo moo. She looked as if she was asleep and peaceful. My brother said a prayer and an elder from our church who accompanied us, gave words. Dad gave the eulogy. Just a few days prior, I listened as he sobbed; but that day, I listened to his strength. Don't get me wrong, in my opinion, tears are not a sign of weakness, they actually represent vulnerability and strength. I find that vulnerability and transparency are often misconstrued or feared and many people avoid them as a result, but I digress. How does one eulogize their own mother with such power? I didn't understand the depth of his pain in those moments, but I knew it had to be hard to give the eulogy for the one person in the world who carried and birthed him.

In the time following the funeral and committal service at the gravesite, we went to a restaurant for the repast. This particular restaurant was a buffet that we had gone to before when visiting. In previous years, I remember eating there with one of my late uncles. The time there brought back memories and thoughts of him. Those who accompanied us traveled back home afterward, and my immediate family stayed an extra day to finish everything and spend more time with our family.

The next morning, we went to Grandma's house one more time before heading back home. When we pulled up to the small house, I thought about how she wouldn't be there–not that time. We wouldn't play Wheel of Fortune, drink Pepsi, or laugh together– not that time. We wouldn't sit at her kitchen table as the trains stormed by and the smoke rose from her ashtray–not that time. Dad would never again drop me off at this house. For me, that experience with her was truly once-in-a-lifetime.

I have witnessed some devastating, sad scenes in my life; and that day, another one of those scenes would be etched in my memory forever. After being at Grandma's house for the final time, sadness swept over me as the pages of this particular chapter in our lives closed. It's always hard to say goodbye to a loved one, especially one with whom you hoped to create more memories because you only had just a few to hold on to. If you've ever lived away from family, when it's time to part, the emotion of sadness is probably not foreign to you. The sadness I felt as a little girl watching Grandma get on her plane was temporary because I was hopeful to see her again. Even though it was temporary, I would miss her. The day after her funeral, it was permanent. There was a heaviness in our midst as these realities set in. I knew I wasn't the only one who felt it.

More than me, her children were left with a void that would never again be filled. We only have one mother. When it came time to get in the car and get on the road, I watched as Dad came out the enclosed porch door. I can picture that moment in my mind even as I write. With tears in his eyes, holding one of his mom's housecoats near his heart, he descended the stairs to begin the journey of life without his mom.

What Dad felt on the inside seeped into the atmosphere as we drove home. As my brother and I were talking the other day, he mentioned to me how quiet Dad was during that drive. I don't remember all the details, but I do recall the solemness of the trip.

Even through the pain of loss, he thought about some of the requirements that needed to be met in order for me to get my driver's license. I had my temporary permit and had driven quite a bit as I spoke about in chapter two, but I needed more hours.

Getting my license was a big deal for me because it meant a little more freedom and independence. I was more than ready and had been for a while. I didn't even know that Dad was thinking about those hours I needed as we traveled home until he or my brother (one of them was driving at the time) pulled the car over and told me to take us home. I was a little shocked. Looking back, if I were my dad, I would've wanted to just get home and prevent any extra extensions of the trip from happening. I'm grateful for him being a selfless, generous, and considerate person.

Upon hearing his instructions, I hesitated for a moment because I was a little tired and confused. After the doors of the car opened, the interior lights shined brightly, and my family rearranged their seats like musical chairs, I quickly got out of the car and hopped into the driver's seat. Dad sat in the passenger's seat while Mom, my brother, and my sister were in the back seat. I had driven his car before on the local highway and through our local city but never on an interstate. I was a smidge intimidated due to not having driven this route before, but I listened to Dad's direction, pulled onto the road, and began driving. He was with me. If I were to take a wrong turn or drive down a path that didn't lead to home, he could answer any questions that I may have had and also guide me.

Before long, Dad fell asleep. He relaxed enough to close his eyes and rest. All the while, Mom sat in the backseat trying to stay awake because I was driving. She once told me that she couldn't believe that Dad slept while I drove us home on that night. The fact that he did, helped her to realize it was okay to do the same. He knew that I could do it, he taught me well, and he trusted me. Eventually, she closed her eyes and rested too. After driving in the weighty silence, we made it home safe and sound.

Four

Therapy or counseling wasn't something that was really discussed or attended in our household when I was growing up. It definitely wasn't frowned upon; I just think my parents weren't exposed to it or it wasn't a norm for them when they were raised. The lack of discussion about therapy leads me to believe it wasn't sought after.

After Grandma died, I don't recall Dad going to grief counseling or anything of the sort. As a matter of fact, I don't think we had many conversations about her death after the funeral, if at all. It could be that I didn't store those memories, but I'm almost certain that it didn't happen. I know Dad told me she died that night in March of 2000. I believe he also asked me how I felt at some point, but not much more comes to mind as I think back to this time.

Considering everything he was going through, trauma was certainly experienced. Dealing with his cancer diagnosis, cancer surgery, blood clots, the death of his mother, and eulogizing her, had to have taken a toll. Not to mention dealing with all of this while still being a husband, father, provider, pastor, brother, teacher, and the list goes on. The lack of attending therapy sessions strikes me as odd because Dad counseled people as a pastor. He knew the importance of counseling, but his faith and relationship with Jesus mended, as well as, sustained him. He was very educated and continuously sought to gain more knowledge. He was equipped with his doctorate in Theology and other degrees; he was just a wise and godly man. He prayed a lot, he preached, and he taught. He also worked a secular night shift job for many years, to sustain and provide for his family. Sometimes, I wonder if there was ever time for him to unpack and work through life with a professional. If there was time, would he then become a target for onlookers (specifically parishioners, peers, or the like) to deem him unfit to do the work God called him to do? Let me pause and clarify something. I've never heard anything like this from him or anyone else. My mind thinks about these things and questions arise that he can no longer answer for me. So, in turn, it leaves me to wonder. It's as simple as that. The concern that I have is that in some instances or church settings, counseling or therapy for the pastor is criticized. If anyone needs this outlet, pastors and leaders do. The tremendous weight that they carry is indescribable.

These leaders are viewed through the lens of people who cannot begin to fathom what it's like to walk in that calling. Yet, the same people will have a whole lot to say about what the leader is doing "wrong" or how they would do it if they, themselves, were in leadership. They saw what they wanted to "see" through a filter of bitterness and unresolved issues within their own lives. I saw how he faithfully labored to lead God's people, not perfect but faithful. I observed how many people loved him and were faithful to him as he was led by God. On the other side of that, I saw how some criticized (sometimes not constructively) and wondered why he did things the way he did. There's always room for questions, comments, concerns, and suggestions but the way something is said usually speaks louder than what is said. Having the right motives also plays a key part in helping or supporting. What probably bothered me the most was how some people lied about him, talked negatively about him, and slandered him. What's crazy is, sometimes they would do it in front of his children. But when they spoke to us, we had to show God's love as if they had done nothing. Yeah, I failed that test on an occasion or two, but it was best for me to literally keep my mouth closed. Some people thought they could do a better job at pastoring so they may have given him a hard time. With that being said, please pray for our leaders instead of being set on stirring up confusion. You may think you can do it better, but you are not the leader, and you're probably not the leader because you think you can do it better. We see leaders who suffer from depression and some have even taken their own lives. We need to be ever so careful to be a part of the solution versus a part of the problem. My dad was not depressed, but I was glad when some relief came his way and he was able to take off one of the many "hats" he wore.

In the summer of 2000, Dad retired from his secular job. We had a big retirement party at our church to celebrate. For quite some time before this, it was his desire to retire. For years, I watched him get off work at 8 on Sunday mornings after working all night. He came home, took a shower, ate breakfast, studied, and sometimes laid down briefly before heading off to teach Sunday school at 10:30. He preached the sermon at the 12-noon service and then went home to eat dinner and finally rest. After briefly resting, we had Sunday night service from 7:30 until between 9 and 9:30. Dad came home, laid down for a little while, and got back up to go to work at midnight.

There was Bible Study on Tuesday nights and Missionary Service on Thursday nights, both at 7:30. If Dad wasn't off work those evenings, he came home after service, just like on Sunday nights, rested for a little while, and went to work at midnight.

These were just regular church services. He also traveled to various churches to preach, oversee, and celebrate other pastors and congregations. There was so much more that he did that I witnessed, but some of it I didn't.

I went alongside Dad to the nursing homes to visit and pray for the sick. I was not fond of going there because I was afraid, but he took me anyway. The thing that sticks out to me the most about going was that Dad had me pray for whomever we were visiting right along with him. He told me specifically what to do, and I did it. As he laid his hand on the person, I was to lay my hand on his back or arm and join him in prayer. After he instructed me in this the first time, I guess it was expected whenever we would go after that. I didn't realize Dad was training me until I became an adult and thought back to these times.

Our house phone rang so much to the point where when our friends or guests came over, some of them would comment about it. I remember telling many callers that Dad was sleeping. It was like I, and whoever picked up the phone, was his secretary. I wrote many messages on paper or committed them to memory to share with him when he woke up. I gently put the messages on the TV tray beside the bed or even posted them on the refrigerator with a magnet. At times, there was an emergency with one of the church members or their family. There were also those who called who obviously couldn't tell the difference between an actual emergency and a call that really could have waited and been a quick conversation later. Either way, I'd have to wake him. I felt bad because he didn't get much rest; but at the same time, I was glad he would be awake because I got to see him.

As a child, I didn't realize just how much dedication and continual sacrifice Dad made for his family and the church. He began to experience burnout doing both. Thankfully, he was able to come off his job and dedicate even more time to the church. It would seem like he had more downtime if he retired; but to me, it was like he became busier. His time shifted from family, church, and a secular job to family and church. He had no therapy, but definitely healing and guidance from God.

As I sit here and write, I think about how much therapy has helped me. I will get into this later, but from what I've experienced, I wish I had the opportunity to speak with my parents about going. I believe it would have helped them to talk about their childhoods or just life. For anyone who knew either or both of my parents, you know that they were the sweetest, genuinely-kind, godly, caring, loving, and all those other wonderful superlatives you would interject, people you could ever meet. God did that, He truly worked wonders in their lives. The pair of them were able to function successfully and do the work of the Lord regardless of their backgrounds. God is our ultimate healer and He is everything we need.

Dad used to say, "God gives us faith, and He also gives us common sense." In its context, he was speaking about taking medication if need be. Exercising your faith shouldn't be reckless. To godly things, there is order. If you know that you need a particular medication for depression or whatever it may be, get it. Of course, you should pray and seek the Lord. Don't be reckless with your health—physical or mental. Sometimes, you have to step out on faith and go to therapy, trusting that God will meet you there and that He will help you put the pieces of His masterpiece together (again and as many times as needed).

I know that God moved mightily in both of my parent's lives. Growing up, I heard true stories about each of their lives, and both of them would bring me to tears. At the same time, I was amazed to see what God made them to be from what once was, truly a miracle.

Their stories (like many others), both individually and collectively, should have been written or told. Let's touch on them briefly, I'll start with Dad.

Dad's mother was a single White woman who gave birth to him in the 1940s, but it wasn't until adulthood that he met his Black father for the first time. He was the oldest of his mother's six children—first five boys and lastly, a baby girl. Over the years, there have been questions about Dad's ethnicity because of his appearance. Some have even mentioned that he looked like he could be Mexican. Simply put, he was mixed with Black and White. His race, or should I say races, by themselves set the stage for him to be an outsider. Where would he fit in or be accepted?

As a child, I looked through family photo albums and various photos stood out to me. One, in particular, captured Dad and three of his brothers when they were very little. They were all turned a little to their left, our right, and they looked like stairsteps. At the top of the stairs was my dad—the only one with curly hair and skin a couple of shades darker than the others. The other photo that stood out to me was of my grandfather, my dad's father. I saw that photo many times, but one day, I learned who he was. He had a tooth that was either all gold or trimmed in gold. He was dressed very finely in a sharp suit. When I found out his name, I can remember scribbling my first name with his last name attached to it to see how it looked. I said it out loud to hear how it sounded. I had never met him because he passed away several years before I was born. I never knew what it felt like to have a grandfather, and my dad never knew what it felt like to grow up and have his father. Despite this lack, he turned out to be one of the best fathers to walk the earth–God did that.

So let's shift our focus to Mom. She was born in the late 1940s to a single Black mother and a mixed (Black, White, and some Indian, I believe) father. When she was around two or three years old, she and her younger sister were left with their maternal grandparents. She called her grandmother, Mama and her grandfather, Daddy. Her grandparents divorced before she turned 10. As a result of the divorce, her grandmother moved out, and Mom was raised by her grandfather. She had to grow up fast and do more for herself because there wasn't a woman in the home. On the weekends, she would go to her great aunt's house; and even though her grandmother didn't live in the home with her, she was very present in her life.

At least once or twice, I asked Mom how she felt about her childhood and the circumstances she faced. She wasn't bitter, nor did she seem to have the capacity to hold a grudge. That spoke volumes to me. Growing up, Mom was content—her basic needs were met. She never expressed feeling bad or sad, nor did she complain. She was raised in a spiritual environment where she was taught not to hold onto negativity and unless you entertained it, it wouldn't take root. She was provided with strong spiritual principles of forgiveness and long-suffering. This stuck with her throughout her life. She was a big help to those attached to her and had the intuition to be there for her older relatives. She helped seniors and everyone she came in contact with if she could–she had the gift of helps. Despite lack, she turned out to be one of the best mothers to walk the earth–God did that.

There is just so much more that I could go into here concerning these two precious people who gave me life, but my reason for sharing this snippet was to show you how God can work in your life no matter your circumstances. You may be surprised by how many people you come into contact with, possibly daily, whose upbringing and pasts don't reflect their lives now. God can take what most people would throw away, ignore or even be ashamed of and use it for His glory. I know this isn't a self-help book, but please allow me to just encourage you to go after God with every fiber of your being. You are at the right place and this is the right time to see His miracles unfold in your life. Sometimes, that starts with therapy.

Five

So, let's rewind just a smidge. I started my first job in the Spring of 1999, months before Dad's diagnosis. I'd just turned 15 and had imagined how fun it would be to work at this specific local custard stand. We frequented it when I was a child and on up through adulthood. So much so, the owner knew Dad's order. She would say, "A black raspberry shake. What size?" As I typed the flavor, I could almost taste it—the nostalgia. Dad and I shared a love for ice cream. He fed it to me for the first time when I was only four or five months old. When I was a small girl, my usual was a small vanilla in a cup topped with plain M&Ms, no cones. I loved how the colors from the little candies bled on the pure white background of the ice cream. I felt like it gave the vanilla a little more flavor. As I got older, my favorite became a Reese's Cup blurry, comparable to a blizzard. It's still my favorite now and the reason for at least a pound or two.

I had a lot of fun and gained a wealth of customer service experience working there. I learned how to make the "perfect" ice cream cone. The owner put her hand over ours while we held the cone to make sure we were properly swirling the ice cream and pulling down at the right time for the top to look tall, all to her

29

standard. I have to admit that it was a little humiliating, especially when someone I knew watched from one of the three ordering windows. So it's safe to say that I gained a little patience there too.

Only girls worked there and we always looked forward to the owner leaving us so we could work a little more freely. It was a rule that we could eat all the ice cream we wanted, as long as we made it in one of the reusable, hard plastic cups in the kitchen. I made myself my favorite blurry and probably consumed too many of them that summer. Even though I enjoyed it, this was a seasonal job. The custard stand opened in April or May and usually closed in September. So I looked for another job after the summer.

In the summer of 2000, not only did Dad retire, I worked at Chuck E. Cheese's throughout. I applied for and received the cashier position, but this wasn't limited to just standing behind the register. A lot of the time, I ran the Kid Check stand, stamping the hands of the parents and the hands of their children with matching letter-number combinations indicating they belonged together upon their leaving. On Saturday mornings, this duty was less than fun because the place would reach capacity and there would be a wait, sometimes a long one. Lines of frustrated, stressed parents with upset, whining children would weave out the door onto the sidewalk and parking lot. When one family or party left, I was able to stamp more people in. It was like a revolving door, but when the door would come to a halt, parents, grandparents, aunties, and uncles questioned me about how much longer it would be. Very rarely, an impatient adult whose child had grown tired of waiting would take the rope down and let themselves in. It was a little unbelievable at times.

If I wasn't taking orders or checking people in, I managed the prize center while working as a cashier. Little children brought their tickets to me and took plenty of time making those ever-so-crucial decisions about which prize or candy they wanted. I observed as parents grew more and more impatient while these decisions were being made, or because they were standing in line waiting for their child's turn. This was another job that required much patience.

Occasionally, I had to wear "the suit." You know what suit I'm speaking of, right? Yes, that one. I had to be Chuck E. two or three times during my stint there. As a child who loved coming to Chuck E. Cheese's, I'd never imagined that I would end up "being" him one day. This was an experience, for sure. Children and some adults either excitedly ran up to me or bolted away from me in terror. Little hands pulled the nose and teeth of the costume, while others poked and prodded at what they thought was an anthropomorphic rat-turned-mouse's body. Unfortunately for me, I could feel all of that while I struggled slightly under the weight of the gigantic head. As I walked around dancing and entertaining the many guests, the smell of compounded sweat and funk from many others who had worn this same costume would do its own dance through my nostrils and make me regret the decision to work there.

I remember getting dropped off at work, but that arrangement didn't last long. One day, I got ready for work and I thought Dad was going to take me. The next thing I knew, he handed me his keys and told me to be careful, I was shocked. I'd driven his car, with him in it, several times before (including the interstate when coming back from Grandma's funeral, just a few months prior), but taking it by myself to work was a new experience. He had a light blue 1997 Lincoln Town Car with a dark navy cloth rag top. It had several bells and whistles that I was super impressed with when he purchased it. I remember thinking, *Dad is letting me take his car to work? He must really trust me.*

My job wasn't too far from our house, but it was far enough away that I took the expressway. I adjusted the mirrors and the seat to my comfort level, cranked on the A/C, turned the radio to the local R&B station because I couldn't listen to it when Dad was in the car (I also didn't own many, if any, cassette tapes to play in the tape deck), and almost float to work because of the ever-so-smooth luxury ride. I'd get lost while driving, not in physical location, but my mind would wander because driving was soothing for me. At the time, my responsibilities outside of our home only included working and when school was back in session, school. I was experiencing a new phase of my life, just as Dad described to me when we recently had gone on one of our dates.

At this point, I'd already experienced having feelings for a young man or two, very limited dating, and what I knew to be love at the time. My parents took very seriously who I interacted with and where I went. My lack of understanding and experience caused me to think they were too strict at times. I've found that in more than a few journal entries, I expressed my dislike for how I wasn't allowed to do certain things or go to certain places. I wanted more freedom and to be treated more like a young adult. You know, I wanted all the typical things most teenagers wanted.

I was always mature for my age, so I had been told. At 16, I thought I was mature. I accredited this to my parents being a little older when they had me and to both of my siblings being nine plus years older than me. Even though my teenage self wanted more freedom, I actually already had quite a bit.

Growing up, I was able to spend the night at some of my best friend's houses. One of my best friends and I were so close that we called each other cousins. Her mom called my dad "Unc" years before either of us was born. It seemed as if she and I had known each other since the womb. We always planned to see how we could get together. Many times, we went to each other's houses between Sunday services. As we became older, this didn't stop.

When I was between 14 and 15 years old, I began to spend time with some of the young ladies who were a few years older than me from church. There were two, in particular, who took up quite a bit of time with me, my best friend/cousin, and some of my other friends. I hadn't known them for long because they were pretty new to our congregation but quickly became close with us. I was amazed at how much time they wanted to spend with me, due to the age gap, but we looked at each other like sisters.

Many weekends, I stayed with them at their apartments. I looked forward to getting out of school on Fridays because I just knew one of them would pick me up for the weekend. We went shopping, out to eat, had game nights, went to the movies, and the list goes on. One particular time we stayed over at one of our houses, there were so many of us in one bed, I don't know how any of us slept. There was so much love, many shared secrets, and immeasurable laughter between all of us. Outside of my family, they were my safe place, at the time.

On Sunday mornings, we turned upbeat gospel music on and cooked breakfast together. Then after we ate, we went to church for Sunday school and service. Frequently after service, a group of us would get together over one of our houses, cook dinner, play games, and hang out before evening service. It seems as if it was this way for years. I like to look back and call that duration the good ole' days. I didn't take that time in my life for granted because some teens didn't and don't have this type of support system while navigating through these fragile and crucial years. I'm grateful that my parents allowed me to leave with them so often. So to my point, I had some freedom.

In the fall of 2000, I was a junior in high school. Every morning, the dreadful sound of that alarm clock going off brought me back to reality from whatever dream that held me captive. My routine was pretty regular—get up, shower, get dressed, fix my hair, eat breakfast, and brush my teeth. Then we, usually my mom and I, headed out, jumped into her minivan, and went up the street to pick up another one of my childhood best friends. After Mom dropped us off at school, she went to work. After school, my dad usually picked us up. This happened day after day until the beginning of November.

On Thursday, November 9, 2000, I got up and went about my day as usual. If I remember correctly, around this time, there had been just a little bit of car-for-me talk going on. However, I didn't anticipate what would happen after school that day. We took a little detour and somehow ended up at a car dealership. I tried to suppress and stop the excitement from bubbling up on the inside because it would soon seep out onto my face. I wanted to play it cool, you know, just in case we were only going to browse. Before getting out of the car, Dad said something along the lines of us just going to see what I liked and what they had. I knew what he said, but I also knew my dad. I'd witnessed him handle business, be charismatic, move under the power of the Holy Spirit, and change atmospheres with his presence. If there was a car for me on that lot and I was supposed to have it at that time, I knew it was mine even if Dad didn't intend to buy it that day. Despite this knowledge, I so badly wanted to drive away from there with a car of my own.

As we looked around, there was one car that stood out to me, but I hesitated to say so. After some time passed, Dad finally asked if I saw a car I liked, so I jumped at the opportunity. He looked over the car I mentioned, and we took it for a test drive. I drove first, Dad second. While we drove, I was so happy and just hoped that this car was it. It wasn't brand new, in fact, it was quite a bit older, but I loved it. I loved it because it was the threshold to growth and new beginnings. The adrenaline made my heart beat a little faster as Dad sped down the highway to "blow out the cobs," as he put it. He put a new meaning behind test driving, but because I was with Daddy, I didn't panic or get scared; I was safe even in that situation. As we sped down the Innerbelt, I just smiled. I felt like the car was already mine.

Upon returning to the dealership, my mind raced with possibilities. *Could this be the day I walk away with a car or would my independent world tarry a little longer?* We took a seat at a car salesman named Frank's desk. As we waited, my dad threw some information out to me about my upcoming college expenses. I intercepted that train of thought as quickly as possible because I didn't want it to stand in the way of my car, so I said, "I'll get scholarships." To which he replied that he hadn't thought about that. My grades were great, I was involved in a couple of clubs, and many opportunities waited for me in the near future. At that point, I saw things looking up for me concerning the car.

Once Frank came to speak with us, Dad offered to pay a price that was a lot lower than what was listed on the windshield. Frank excused himself to speak with whomever he needed to about our offer. Meanwhile, Dad looked at me and said, "I don't think they're going to go for that." His words echoed my thoughts but if it was mine, it was mine. I rested in that fact.

The wait felt way longer than it actually was. When I woke up and went through my routine that morning, I didn't know I would find myself at a car dealership awaiting the possible news that would change my life. When Frank returned, he came bearing words that did just that. Needless to say, I was ecstatic!

We scheduled to come back the next day to complete the purchase and pick up the car. Just as Dad handed me the keys to his car with trust, he handed me the keys to my burgundy 1993 Buick Skylark—the feeling was unexplainable. He told me that he would see me at home, made sure I got into the freshly washed car safely, and I drove off. I had waited for this specific freedom for so long. To be able to go grab something to eat or go anywhere without having to wait for a ride meant a lot. I sat there for just a minute to soak it all in before driving off into a new chapter of my life.

When I got home, I parked in the driveway, still in disbelief. I turned the car off, locked my door, and before I could walk toward the house, Dad was out there ready to pray over the car. He laid his hands on it and prayed; I will never forget it. That day will forever be etched into my memory as one of the best days ever. Daddy loved to give good gifts.

I was so appreciative to my parents for the car and their trust. I have always been one to express myself through some type of writing, so I wrote them a letter. It wasn't just any letter as I penned it pretty creatively and presented it to them so they would know just how much their generosity meant to me.

A few days later, I was hesitant to drive myself to church. My parents reassured me that it was fine, so I drove to church for the first time in my new car—excited and a little nervous. I pulled into the parking lot, parked, and went into the building as I usually would.

Now for the reason I was hesitant: In my experience, as a PK (many refer to this as a preacher's kid, but mine stands for pastor's kid–two totally different things and roles), not only is the pastor scrutinized, but his or her family is also. In our case, not just from some (it wasn't everyone) in our local congregation but also from other members of our church organization. As I mentioned before, Dad was a bishop or overseer of various churches. It's pretty sad some of the things we endured while in this role. People place you under a microscope and find fault with *your* family but can't find fault within their own. Why is this? Why do people put pastors and their families on pedestals only to tear them down? Then they create an impossible standard (that's not even biblical) by which they want the first family to live. When the family isn't perfect, does it give the onlookers a loophole to not live up to what's being preached? As I said, it's pretty sad and unfortunate, but what's sadder is that I'm sure I am not speaking from a solo experience. Many PKs and their families have similar stories.

There were things that we endured as a family that, I believe, could be coined as abuse. From slander, to gossip, to outlandish assumptions and flat-out lies, we have seen, felt, and heard. There was a specific time when we attended a combined church picnic. My dad didn't come with us to this particular one. Some of the young people (young teens through young adults) were playing kickball. A girl from a different church purposely and violently launched the ball at my sister's head as she ran to a base. After the hit, the girl proceeded to brag and laugh about how she did so. This particular girl came from a long line of women who enjoyed drama, who had jealous spirits, and who, for no particular reason, didn't care for my sister or me. So as you see, this was not an isolated incident. My sister simply laughed it off knowing that retaliation wasn't an option. Even though she didn't want to let it go, she thought the better of it because she was the bishop's daughter and did not want to bring scorn to our daddy's name. When it happened, our mother was furious because their pastor did nothing about it. She had us pack everything up and we left the picnic early.

That is just one of what feels like a countless number of examples. I could write another book about the PK experience. I found it difficult to be my authentic self, let my hair down, or fully enjoy certain things because of what would be perceived or said. As a young adult, I struggled with the weight of church people's opinions of me, but I am so glad that I eventually allowed Christ to free me of what others thought and said about me. At this point, I sense the Holy Spirit directing me to remind you that His opinion (which is truth) of you, and His thoughts toward you are what count. Not even your own negative thoughts can redirect the thoughts that your Daddy has about you. No matter what your life experience has been up until this point, He still says you are called, chosen, loved, and purposed. This will never change.

So, back to my car and church. I went into the building and it was a normal service or Bible Study. Dad must have mentioned to the congregation that he had bought my car. I'm thinking that he did this to somewhat prevent questions that may have come my way about the car. At this point, I can't be certain, but I do know what I heard when I walked to my car after church. "Let me go over here and see what my tithes dun' paid for." *Excuse me? Did I just hear right?* So in my position as a PK, I was probably not supposed to say anything or maybe I was supposed to fakely laugh it off. However, this rude comment was upsetting and I didn't resist the urge to say part of what was on my mind. Before I knew it, words began to fly out of my mouth. I said something along the lines of the church not paying my dad enough to be able to buy me a car. I also added that he'd just retired not long ago. I could not believe what I had heard but at the same time, I could.

Let me take a minute to explain what happens in some churches. Of course, I can't speak for all, but I will tell you what my experience has been like and what I have seen. Because some pastors or preachers have been known for taking or stealing money from the church that's not rightfully theirs via salary or gifts, other preachers/pastors, who don't do this, wrongfully obtain a bad reputation. I feel the need to interject that my dad never had that reputation. He was one of the most honest people who didn't play about God, his family, the church, or the church's money, and our congregation knew that. We didn't have hundreds or thousands of members in our church, so what was collected from those who tithed or gave offerings hadn't been enough to sustain the church *and* our family. This was the reason Dad pastored and worked a job on top of that for many years before this time. The person who made this remark could have very well been trying to joke with me, but there are some things you just don't say. I don't know if this is true in every situation, but I've heard that when someone jokes about something, there may be a little truth behind it. Joking or not, I didn't appreciate the comment and it was super unnecessary.

When your tithes/offering leaves your hands, you're done with it. You have done your part and God will bless you for giving back what belongs to Him. (Furthermore, if a person is that concerned about "their" money being mishandled, is it possible that they may need to go and sow into another ministry? Food for thought.) You are not responsible for what's done with it after that. You've been obedient to the Lord. Because some people didn't have this mindset, I felt at times I couldn't fully enjoy certain things, my car included. After some time, the newness wore off and the feeling eventually ceased. I was finally able to appreciate my freedom and newfound independence.

Six

There are so many memories of Dad's cancer journey that they often run together. Not long after he bought my car, he underwent some radiation treatments. This took place from approximately November 2000 to January 2001. If I understood him correctly, Dad told me he would go through radiation after the surgery just in case the doctors didn't get all the cancerous cells. I feel like he shielded me from what was happening because I extensively documented everything in my journals; however, I didn't write about his journey for several months. I also didn't understand why there was such a long stretch from the time of the surgery in February to the time of radiation in November.

One day around this time, I sat in Spanish class when an office worker came in and handed me a call slip. They either verbally told me to hurry up because there was a family emergency, or it was written on the slip. I felt the blood rush from my face as I popped up out of my seat. It felt like people around me could visibly see my heart beating because I thought it would beat out of my chest. I went through so many emotions as I flew out of the classroom. There was a rule–no running in the hallways. This had to be one of those exception-to-the-rule sort of situations. I walked as quickly as

I could with the palms of my hands on either side of my head, due to the state of panic I put myself in. I hit a light jog as I approached the stairs, but once I started descending, my feet felt like they couldn't move fast enough. *Lord please, I can't lose my daddy.* Different tragic scenarios played through my mind to prepare me for something I wasn't ready for. As I finally made it down all the stairs and turned the corner to enter the main hallway, there Dad stood with a smile on his face. He had to have seen the anxiety and sheer worry written all over my face because he immediately said he didn't mean to scare me. *Welp, too late.* I had to recover and calm myself down. Do you know what my lovely daddy told me he wanted? Some type of way he locked himself out of the house. His good friend brought him to my school to get my house key. I was relieved but done. I wanted to laugh, cry, and scream from relief all at the same time. I gave him my house key and proceeded to take myself back to class very slowly so I could process and get over what happened. I can somewhat laugh about it now, but "family emergency" wasn't a term that was used loosely, so I just knew Daddy was laid up somewhere on this side of heaven or the better side. The lesson I received from this came many years later. God would bring it back to my remembrance as an adult. I was all worried and upset that day and had no reason to be. How often have we worked ourselves up over what was said, the unknown, or our thoughts? We allow our emotions to take us all over the place when all we need to do is trust God and know that it will work out.

The fall of 2001 began my senior year in high school–this was a pretty busy year. I took two classes at my high school–one required for graduation and the other an elective which was like a work-study class. I also took two courses at the local university (post-secondary options). During my senior year and the previous summer, I worked downtown as a clerical intern for the city of Akron, thanks to the work-study program. In addition, I was senior class president, so there were meetings and planning sessions that contributed to my busy schedule.

One day, I was in my work-study class. It felt like an ordinary day until the TV was turned on. Suddenly, everyone's attention was drawn to it as we watched the disaster of the twin towers and the attack on America unfold before our eyes. I was scheduled to leave the high school to go to the university for a class right after that, but I wasn't so sure if that was the right thing to do. Uncertain, I went anyway. I sat at my desk among a few other concerned individuals; most of the class didn't show. The heaviness of what had happened hovered in the atmosphere. All of a sudden, lights flashed and the alarm system alerted us to evacuate the building as the university was shutting down. As I hurried to my car, the thought of going to the church instead of home came to my mind. I thought my dad would be there as the church was undergoing a partial remodel.

There were several cars in the parking lot when I pulled through the gates of the church. I went into the building and a few people were working. My eyes kept searching until I found the person I'd come to be around–the one who was my safe and secure place– Dad. I knew that once I saw him, I was good. My brother also had the idea to come to the church from his prior location because he arrived around the same time. When the cares of this life made way for worry, when the stress of it all seemed overwhelming, when uncertainty plagued my mind, or when I needed to feel love tangibly, I could always find solace in my parents.

As graduation grew closer, it was on my heart to bring baccalaureate back. This ceremony was something that hadn't been done at my high school for several years, but I had the urge to reestablish it. The government had already taken prayer out of schools, but this would not keep us from praying. Teachers could not lead us in prayer, but during my junior year, one of my teachers asked me to head up and lead the prayer around the flagpole. I was honored. Baccalaureate was also something, like the prayer at the pole, that may have been frowned upon due to it being spiritual in nature, but I realized how much we needed it. I also knew the perfect person to give the farewell sermon or speech to our graduating class–my dad!

I had written about him as my hero in my 11th-grade honors English class. He was the example of godliness assigned to me to show and teach me the ways of the Lord. I would be remiss if I considered someone else whose life I didn't have a "front-row" seat to witness. Throughout my life, I watched Dad selflessly dedicate himself to the Kingdom of God. The crazy thing is, there was much more that I didn't have the pleasure of witnessing because he dedicated his life to Christ years before I was born. But, I observed as he walked through some of the most trying times of his life. He walked with God, he cried out to God, and he put his trust in God. I knew Dad would give our graduating class a relevant and timely word to aid us in our new beginning.

Dad worked on his speech/sermon and asked me for my opinion on some of it. He had preached countless sermons but had never done this before, so it was new territory. At one point between the awards ceremonies, private scholarship dinners, and recognitions through that school year, he looked at me and said that I'd taken him to places he'd never been before. That small yet profound statement meant so much to me. I was just glad to have him and Mom there to cheer me on and offer support at various events. I truly couldn't have done it without them.

Baccalaureate was another one of those "places" he had never been. I was honored to give my two cents on his address. As he worked on his speech, I worked on mine for graduation. Sunday afternoon, June 2, 2002, this beautiful ceremony took place. Dad did not disappoint as he gave a wonderful address and prayed over our graduating class. He was proud of me, but this day among many other days, I was proud of him. Inadvertently, he taught me to embrace new challenges and navigate unfamiliar territory without fear. He was my daddy, he could do anything.

The next day, June 3, 2002, I stood tall, although nervous, and addressed my fellow graduates, just as Dad did the previous day. I spoke about how we had endured much as a class but how we had gotten to the other side of it. That day, I graduated 6th in the class out of 168, with honors. As that part of my life closed, I reflected upon what it took to get there. High school wasn't really fun for me, so I looked forward to moving on from it and not having to deal with some of what I endured any longer. As a new chapter of life opened to me, I embraced it and looked forward to reading what it said.

Seven

The year 2002 not only held my high school graduation but also held the news of Dad's elevated cancer levels which indicated that the surgeons nor the radiation were successful in eliminating all the cancer. As I stated before, I believe there was a level of protection that Dad shielded over me concerning everything that happened to him. I say this because he has been informed, at that point, that it was incurable due to its spread. Dad didn't, nor did anyone else, share this with me. I knew he had to undergo various treatments, but I thought doctors were still hopeful of there being a chance to rid his body of it, not just attempt to extend his life. We were in the thick of a fight that I thought we could have won.

That year, Dad's cancer was first treated with hormone therapy to reduce and slow the spread. The doctor said that he had some patients whose lives were prolonged for about 10 years using the same treatment. The doctor also mentioned that he wouldn't have done anything differently concerning the surgery two years prior, the disease was just aggressive. I only knew he was going through treatment; I didn't know we were fighting an uphill battle or that through treatment, the inevitable was being prolonged.

In the fall, I started college full-time at the same local university at which I completed my post-secondary classes. My internship with the city also came to an end as it was a program for high school seniors. A few days into the semester, I remember sitting at the dining room table telling my mom that I didn't know if college was for me. She was very calm and told me that she supported whatever decision I made, but she also encouraged me to give it a little more time because it was just the beginning. I don't know what came over me, but I just felt like I wanted to do something else with my life. I continued without knowing what it was, because I had no other plan. I just knew I wanted more than what I was currently contemplating. Despite those feelings, I ended the semester well. I came out with As and Bs and looked forward to finishing college as soon as I could.

During this time, my dad told me something that I would hold onto for years to come. There were many things that Dad told me that I held onto and can still hear some of them play in my mind in his voice. However, this particular thing was random, or so I thought at the time. He told me not to approach or pursue men, but rather to let them approach me. I was 18 years old and had already dated some. I'd never approached any of those gentlemen except one. I don't know what was different about him, but time proved that I shouldn't have pursued him first. I guess Dad felt like I might start dating more seriously at that time in my life or because I was legally an adult, something could come from it. I wasn't so sure at the time and as I said, it felt pretty random, but I would soon see that Dad's words were right on time.

What seemed like days after Dad's advice, or should I say mandate, someone caught my eye. At the very end of December 2002, after a service, I was walking up the backstairs of our church and he was coming down the stairs; it was just the two of us. As I ascended, I thought, *Oh, he is cute.* Right after that, I heard Dad in my ear, "Don't you approach him. Let him pursue you." At that same moment, my heart sank because I wanted to say more than a passing and courteous "hello." I wanted him to pursue me. I didn't know much about him other than who he worked for, yet I wanted him to approach me. I didn't even know his name. For a split second, I was tempted to allow my desire to override my obedience. But because I held Daddy in such high regard and because I knew he was right, I opted to be obedient. I kept walking instead of initiating a conversation.

Shortly after walking away, I started helping a friend clean up in the church sanctuary. I was attempting to take my mind off the gentleman when I saw another good friend of mine at the back of the sanctuary waving almost frantically for me to come that way. He was a co-worker of the "staircase guy," so I immediately knew what he wanted and I became nervous. I waved for him to come to the front of the church while I was cleaning up instead of me deserting my post. As he made his way there, I told my girl what he was going to say. Sure enough, I was right. The guy (for the sake of anonymity, let's call him Jon) who caught my eye was also interested in me and wanted my phone number. I let my friend know that I would be downstairs to talk to him and give him my number as soon as I finished. I hurried downstairs, but not for the reason you may think. I rushed down there to find my mom and sister. They were in one of the rooms in the church basement preparing for the church winter recreation set to happen days later. Since there were many people downstairs eating, I was able to slide into the room without my friend or Jon seeing me. I told my mom and sister what happened and they asked if I was going to give him my number. I wasn't sure because he looked quite a bit older than me and I didn't know if Dad would approve. I sat by the wall, flush with the door so I wouldn't be seen if anyone looked into the door's window. Eventually, I found the courage (that I thought I had on those stairs) to give him my number. Even though I was considered an adult, I still didn't know if I would have permission to date him because of the assumed age difference.

Before getting into all the formalities of parental introductions and such, I had to make sure I wanted to get to know him. To do this, I had to talk to him. Not much time passed between giving him my number and his calling. Our many conversations were good, we enjoyed talking to each other, and we both wanted things to continue to progress. However, I was very adamant about getting my parents' approval in order to move forward.

One day, I tried to work up the courage to talk to Dad about setting up a time to meet Jon. I wanted it to work out so badly that I was terrified to talk to him because he may have told me "no." This was new territory for me. I'd gone out on dates before and even had a boyfriend or two in the past, but I knew that this was different. Never had I dated someone who was that much older than me. I forgot to mention that during one of our conversations, I asked him his age, he was 25. I knew he looked older, not old, but older than anyone I'd "talked" to before, and I didn't think that Dad would go for it. I expressed this to him and to my surprise, he had already casually and briefly spoken with my dad the night I saw him on the stairs. Since he had expressed his interest to our mutual friend that night, while I ducked and dodged, our mutual friend introduced him to Dad. I was shocked to hear this and even more shocked to hear Dad's response to his interest. Dad told him that I was 18 and that I was grown. From that, he continued to move forward in his pursuit of me.

A few weeks later, I sat outside of Dad's office in the basement of our house trying to formulate the perfect words to present to him to obtain my desired outcome. I wanted this to work. I liked this guy a lot, but the fear was immobilizing. So I sat there in that La-Z-Boy chair for what seemed like an hour. Then I walked to the office door, which was partially open. I stood there, trying to get the words to come out of my mouth, but they wouldn't. I stood, my heart pounded. Dad wasn't looking in my direction because the door was somewhat behind him and to his side a bit. I felt like he could sense I was there either through seeing me with his peripheral vision or maybe hearing the almost absent rustle of my movement. I stood longer, trying to utter words that refused to surface. Then I slowly turned around, walked over to the chair, and quietly sank into it. As the recliner gave me a gentle squeeze, I rehearsed what I would say in my mind. I tried to calm myself down and get to the root of my feelings. I could only focus on the fear, not on the reality of who I knew Dad to be.

He was Dad. He wasn't mean and always let me know that I could talk to him about anything. He was approachable, kind, and reasonable. But there I sat, letting uncertainty get the best of me. The possibility of not seeking his approval and just dating Jon versus talking to Dad about it, crossed my mind. Various outcomes and thoughts swirled in my mind when all of a sudden, I heard Dad's voice break through the noise, "Mese, is there something you want to talk to me about?" I froze. My heart tried to escape my chest. *Gulp. He did know I was there.* I told him that I did and he told me to come on into his office. I got up ever so slowly, breathed ever so deeply, and walked ever so nervously, over to the door. As I stood there, he turned and looked at me and asked me what was up, ever so casually. I didn't even know how to start this conversation. I began telling him what was on my mind, but as I spoke, tears formed and all that fear rolled down my cheeks. Dad looked almost confused. I kept talking through it, shaky voice and all. After the brief conversation, he told me to set it up and to tell the young man to come over. He was so laid back about it and even remembered who Jon was from that night. If I recall correctly, he threw in a "That wasn't so bad, was it?" I felt much lighter as relief swept over me like a refreshing cool breeze on a hot summer day. I'd worked myself up. I created this space that I never had to be in, all for Dad to be who I already knew he was.

A few days later, I was at work. I worked for a portrait studio and at times, it was quiet because no appointments were scheduled. This particular evening, it was quiet and close to closing time, so I began shutting the studio down to prepare to go home. My phone rang and it was Jon. He said, "Guess where I just left." Puzzled, I didn't guess correctly; so he told me he had just left my house. I thought he was joking because I was at work and he knew it. I wondered why he was at my house without me being there. I inquired further and to my surprise, he had been there speaking with my dad about his intentions and receiving permission to date me.

My mind meandered to a time, not that long before, Dad showed me this paper he had. It was entitled, "Application for Permission to Date My Daughter." I don't remember how he got it, but it was sort of a joke, or so I thought. While Jon briefed me on the phone about his evening with my dad, I wondered if, at any point, that application had been given to him to fill out and return. I figured if he were calling me, all was well, so I let it pass. He asked me if I would go out with him on our first official date that night. Once he received Dad's blessing, he told my parents his plans to take me out right after I got off work and they were good with it. I have to admit, I called home to be sure. My parents assured me that Jon had just left and was coming to meet me after work.

To say I was happy seems like quite an understatement. I was impressed, especially once we sat down for dinner and heard about what transpired while I was at work. I wanted to know all the details: how long he'd been there, how he knew where I lived, what questions were asked, and so on. When I'd left for work, Dad was knee-deep in making his homemade beef stew. He chopped celery and carrots and onions and I don't know what else. This recipe had been passed down to him by his grandmother, whom he lived with for some of his adolescent to young adult years. Dad had the recipe memorized and none of us knew it. Only once every couple of years would we have the privilege of this dish gracing our lips. At one point during their conversation, Dad stirred the huge pot of stew and asked Jon how old he was. When Jon replied that he was 25, Dad seemed to, with the clank of the spoon hitting the stove, teleport from the pot to the chair right in front of Jon. He looked him in the eye and said, "So we're talking man to man." My eyes got big and we cracked up. My admiration for him grew because he didn't even wait for me to set up a time for them to meet, he took it into his own hands and that let me know he was serious about me and wanted to go about things as I did too. We talked, laughed, and enjoyed each other's company. This was the first of many dates and good times spent together.

Our relationship was different from any other I had been in, or I should say he was different from any other guy that I'd "talked" to. This was my first adult relationship. There were times I came home from work to find Jon there with my dad playing "Who Wants to be a Millionaire" on my PlayStation, talking or watching TV. The two of them had a really good relationship. It was like Jon became a part of the family.

One day, Dad asked me about going on a double date. I was thinking, *With who?* Despite my initial reservations (for no real reason except I thought it wasn't cool), we set it up. Dad was always competitive when it came to games and some sports, so on that bowling double date, he did some trash talking and he wanted to win. He and my mom were on a team against Jon and me. Dad bought concessions for everyone. We ate, had good conversations, laughed, bowled, and had a wonderful time. I didn't know what to expect from the evening, but I knew my parents were awesome people. They had proven to me yet again, just how cool they were. Growing up, it didn't always feel like they were cool and it wouldn't at times after that day, but all-in-all, they were.

I accompanied Jon to his hometown to meet his mother and a lot more of his family. I had only spoken to his mother on the phone before this. Everyone was nice and welcoming. Not long after meeting his family, Jon met a lot of my family. His mother later traveled to my house to meet my parents. My parents traveled with me in support to attend Jon's grandfather's funeral. My mom spoke with his grandmother on the phone a few times. I stayed with his grandmother in her home a few times as well. Our relationship was progressing nicely and we were in love. Everyone around us could see that. It was so apparent to the point where people would compliment us. Dad teased Jon from time to time–"My daughter has your nose wide open! You could drive a semi through it!" Jon smiled so hard and nodded in agreement. I was embarrassed.

The day before Mother's Day that year, Jon and I were at the mall. The gift I wanted to give my mom had already been chosen and purchased by me. Jon, on the other hand, searched the mall to find the perfect gift for her from him. He put so much thought into what he wanted to get her and did not stop until he found it–a beautiful and delicate crystal figurine displaying a pair of hummingbirds drinking nectar from a purple flower between them, parts of it trimmed in gold. The time he took and everything about the process that I'd witnessed, was so precious to me. Mom ended up loving it and placed it in her china cabinet.

Even though we had some really good times, we ran into some hiccups along the way. Each time, seemingly conquering them, we continued in our relationship. We explored marriage. We made plans for our future, looked at engagement rings, toured homes, and just knew that this was it. We were going to be together for the rest of our lives.

Eight

My high school's class of 2003 invited Dad back to give their class the baccalaureate address. He accepted the invitation and had a blueprint for what he would say from my class' address the year before. He also began golfing that same summer. He golfed as often as he could, most times with some of the deacons and friends from the church, and sometimes, he would go alone. He picked it up rather quickly and it became therapeutic for him, especially with everything he experienced in his body. He had good days and not-so-good days.

Jon and my relationship grew more serious–it was to the point that Jon asked my parents for my hand in marriage and they approved. I didn't know it at the time but later found out. I was only 19 years old, Dad wasn't completely well, and I wasn't sure about leaving him or home. Jon was set to move back to his hometown soon. As much as I loved him, I couldn't leave my daddy and didn't see how our relationship would work with us being so far apart. So, I ended it…

Talk about sadness–I was beyond sad, I was devastated. It was the end of the summer and he was not only gone from me physically but relationally as well. I continued to work and get myself prepared for my second year of college, but I was grieving and was unaware of the process taking place. One day, Dad asked me what was going on. I felt so bad because I knew Dad liked Jon, but I had to tell him that we were no longer together. He could see the pain I was in and said, "How do you feel?" I knew Dad was already going through a lot, so I quoted myself, "People come and people go." That was a motto that I learned pretty early on because I had a tendency to attach myself to people not realizing they were temporary in my life. After this happened one or two good times, I began to live by this motto. Dad then replied, "That's cold Mese." I just explained to him that I was protecting myself because people aren't permanent. He understood and probably recognized I was partly putting on a brave face for him. I wasn't thinking about the fact that I didn't need to put on a brave face for Daddy. He was my protector and my safe place. If I wanted to completely break down and do the ugly cry on his shirt, I could have. He was not temporary; He was my constant. He was there to comfort me, reassure me, and teach me. I didn't have to be brave for him, he was my hero. At the time, I didn't consider it though. I did not want to talk about it. I wanted to suppress the hurt and just move on with life. Time would heal my wounds, or would it?

That same month, August 2003, we went on a family vacation. We traveled through Philadelphia to Atlantic City, and finally to Washington, D.C. We stopped in Philly to eat authentic Philly Cheesesteaks, view the Liberty Bell, and spend a few hours touring the city before heading to Atlantic City. I had been to the ocean before and walked on the beach, even taken a cruise, but I had never gotten into the ocean. I looked forward to doing so there and was excited about experiencing it, especially with my family.

Once we arrived in Atlantic City, we ate good food, saw famous sites, and took lots of pictures. It was super hot and we walked a lot, up and down the boardwalk. Dad did extremely well on this trip–he didn't get too tired. One particular day, we rented chairs and an umbrella at the beach, sat there, and relaxed. This day stands out to me–the most out of the whole trip–because we actually got into the ocean and had a great time. I stayed within a certain water depth range, one that I was comfortable with, and I had no intentions of leaving that place of comfort. As the waves came crashing in, I jumped so that they wouldn't knock or force me down. Wave after wave, I jumped and jumped. All of a sudden, I looked way out into the water and there was Dad. Then he called out to me, "Mese, come on out here!"

I knew about ocean drop-offs and how they could be anywhere in the ocean. I understood that the ocean floor was not flat and could be higher or lower in certain areas. BUT because he was my daddy, I began to venture out to him, out into the deep. Daddy wouldn't let anything happen to me and I was safe, even in the deep, even without knowing how to swim, just because I was with him. He encouraged me along the way and once I got to him, it wasn't so bad. The water was deep and at times, it would go from my shoulders and neck down to my waist even with me standing in the same area. I waved back at Mom, who was nestled comfortably in her chair under the umbrella. She had enough of ocean when, in water up to her knees, she was knocked down by a wave. My brother was in the ocean but not as far out as we were. As waves came our way, we jumped, laughed, and enjoyed each other. It was quite a workout, but nothing could replace the memories we were creating. Suddenly, I heard Dad yell, "Mese, watch out!" When I turned around, I saw one of the most frightening things for me at that time. I stared up into the face of a wave so huge that I couldn't jump over it, so I knew I was about to go under and it would be bad. It seemed as if time slowed down at that moment.

Have you ever seen the movie *Cast Away* with Tom Hanks? It's one of my favorites. There was a scene in which Tom Hanks' character was trying to get off a deserted island. He got out so far but there was a huge wave that formed and not only went over him, it took him out. The force of the wave pushed him down so deep, he collided with a coral reef where his leg was severely punctured causing such great distress that he screamed under the water. The scene will make you cringe and possibly hold your breath as it unfolds. So there I stood, not able to escape the inevitable, I just had to endure it. I filled my lungs with the biggest breath I could possibly fill them with, not knowing when I would be able to take another. The strength of the tower-like wave was so violent when it collided with my body, I ended up knocked down to a somewhat lying-down position on the seafloor with seaweed ticking my body as thoughts like, *This might be the way I see Jesus face to face*, plagued my mind. I couldn't be certain that I was close to Daddy. I could not hear him any longer. All I heard was the muffled sounds of being underwater and my inward struggle to continue holding my breath. I couldn't feel him, nor could I see him or anything else under the murky, sand-filled water. I prayed that when I attempted to stand up after my struggle, my head would emerge from the depths of the water. If not, and if Dad couldn't find me or wasn't near, I was in trouble.

I stood up. My head came out of the water and I was able to breathe again. Wiping my face and catching my breath, I could hear Dad calling me. He was there and going to rescue me. He asked if I was okay and told me that the wave was a big one. I was relieved and more than okay because I was reassured that even in those moments when all of my senses told me I was alone, he was there.

Needless to say, I was done with my "in the deep" adventures and went back to where I was comfortable. We had a conversation about this once I reached my brother and my mother. Mom remarked about how far out we were and how she didn't think I was going to go out there. I was even able to laugh about it with them. It was an experience I will never forget if I can help it.

We continued the vacation in Washington, D.C. a day or two later. The hotel was very nice; it had a rooftop pool and beautiful rooms. Mom and I took pictures of each other posing and having fun in the room. As she took my picture, I smiled; however, deep down inside, the hurt of the breakup still lingered. As I posed, sitting in the chair, my mind wandered back to Jon and how much I missed him. I breathed deeply and compelled whatever emotions that tried to surface, back down. I wanted to enjoy all of these moments with my family without grief having its way.

Atop the roof, we went swimming. It would seem like I would've been done with water on this trip. Since there were no waves to take me out, I was good. I especially admired and thought about how cute my parents were as I watched them. Mom was afraid of water. I mean she was fearful of even putting her face in the water. For her to get into the pool was a great step. My dad was very playful and knew how to swim well. You saw him in the pool one moment and the next, you wouldn't. You would, however, hear Mom screaming at the top of her lungs, "Ronnie! Ronnie! Stop Ronnie!" as Dad's whereabouts would be made known–he was underwater intent on grabbing Mom's foot or leg. That scared her so much. My brother, Dad, and I cracked up. If anyone knew my mother, you also knew how she was not a loud person. She was calm and soft-spoken but not in that situation. Occasionally, Dad did this, but Mom quickly caught on. If she didn't see him on the surface of the pool, she knew what he was up to and made her way out.

We toured the District on a tourist trolley, getting out to visit the chosen landmarks. One stop was the Lincoln Memorial area. We walked to the Vietnam Veterans' Memorial Wall where I helped Dad look up the name of a friend of his who was killed while they served in the Marine Corps together. We found his name on the wall and I took a picture of Dad kneeling on one knee beside it, pointing at it.

We walked over to the Lincoln Memorial, took photos, and proceeded to the trolley stop. We waited for the trolley with a small crowd of people standing with us as the heavens seemed to open up and an unexpected downpour of rain drenched us. People ran to seek shelter at the little trolley information booth. It did not protect them because the rain seemed to fall sideways too. The Lincoln Memorial was far enough away that it didn't matter if we ran to it, we would still be soaked upon getting there. So the four of us stood, holding sad little rain-soaked fans over our heads, our clothes and hair completely saturated with water, waiting for the trolley to finally come. What a time to not have a strong umbrella or covering.

The rain began to lighten up quite a bit, but the damage had already been done. When the trolley pulled up, we rang out the parts of our clothes that we could and boarded. All the way to Union Station, we sat in our sopping wet clothes, laughed a little, and were ready to get dry. We walked through the freezing Union Station to our car and went back to the hotel. This trip was one of the most memorable family trips we've ever taken. Unbeknownst to us, it would be the last.

During the following fall of 2003, I started my second year of college. My course load was full and I continued to work for the same portrait studio. I still hadn't completely dealt with my grief, nor did I know that I needed to. As I sat in one of my college classes, my professor lectured and I couldn't seem to focus; I could hear him, but I wasn't listening. I gave such an effort to zone into class, but all I could think about was Jon. I told myself things like, *Don't you do it. You better not let one tear fall. You are in the middle of class. Stop it!* Despite these attempts, one tear fell. I fought to hold back. Then another fell and another until finally, I quickly got up to excuse myself from the auditorium of people, sobbing to the exit. I left campus to deal with myself. I knew I would no longer carry sadness one day, I just didn't know when or how to overcome it other than letting time pass.

During this semester and closer to the winter time, Dad underwent chemotherapy. His doctor also prescribed medication to control his pain. On the cold, January evening of Dad's 60th birthday, we went to my workplace to take family photos and out to eat afterward. Dad hadn't taken his pain medicine at home nor did he have any of it with him. He had a hard time while sitting at the table–it was difficult to watch. Frequently, he would groan and squirm under the pressure of the pain. We ended dinner early because Dad's pain intensified and he needed to get home to take his meds.

A few months later in 2004, possibly close to or in the summer, his doctor prescribed a pain patch instead of the pills. He thought it best since the pills began to offer less and less relief. The patch would provide slow, time-released delivery of medicine to be absorbed into his skin. These helped Dad a lot and he was able to get out and enjoy golfing a little when the weather eventually transitioned. His pain was better controlled, but he was still sick and not able to do everything he once did. So when my alma mater's class of 2004 invited him to give the baccalaureate address in June, he thought that he should skip it that time. He asked for my opinion. Having witnessed his good and not-so-good days, I agreed with him. One of those not-so-good days was three months prior in February–he was asked to deliver the eulogy at a friend's graveside service. He pushed himself through his sickness to do it because of the relationship and history he had with their family. He didn't want to disappoint. The thing is, like with most families, our family saw what others did not see. It was a bitterly cold day, snow and ice covered the ground. Dad drove to the funeral with my mom, and I accompanied them. I watched as he gave what seemed like everything he had to deliver the eulogy and appeal to the audience on behalf of Jesus Christ. But when it was over, I saw the toll it took on his body. Upon returning to our car, he handed me the keys as he was too weak to even make the nine-minute commute home. As he crawled into the back and lay across the cold, blue leather seats, he looked so exhausted. As I drove home, I glanced back and Dad was laying in the seat to find relief in rest. My heart sank. I know he sacrificed many days for friends, but sitting out for the baccalaureate address this year was a wise decision.

At some point during this period, my brother took Dad to get his first cell phone. It was funny listening to him talk on it. He didn't realize that a cell phone picked up and amplified your voice much more than a landline phone. So we could hear his conversation, most of the time from both ends, as he spoke so loudly on his new gadget. He thought it was so neat. To keep his phone from ringing all of the time, ultimately protecting him, everyone did not have his number. Many times, when we called him, he was on the golf course. It was great to see him enjoying his life, despite the circumstances. We always knew God was able to heal his body, no matter what. So life continued to be lived.

Nine

The summer of 2004 was truly a life-changing time. It was one in which Dad underwent radiation and also liquid chemotherapy as his health continued to decline slowly but definitely noticeably. He continued pastoring and pouring into people through his sickness. He also golfed whenever he felt good enough to go, and a time or two, he went even though he wasn't feeling the greatest. The scenery and the game did something for him and helped him through.

On Thursday, June 17, 2004, the world as I knew it took on a completely different meaning. The bathroom in the basement of my house is where my body shook and my heart pounded violently in my chest as I waited for my pregnancy test results. I took deep breaths in an attempt to slow what seemed to be adrenaline taking control of my nerves. My thoughts wouldn't stop no matter how many times I told myself *everything will be fine.* Yes, ultimately everything would be fine, but what would my family and I have to endure to get to *fine? What will people say? How am I going to provide for my child? My parents–how will I tell Daddy? Daddy. He's sick, this is going to…*then…it was time to look. So, I looked and found out I was a mother. I could say I found out I was going to be a mother but for me, the moment I found out, I already was one. I was nervous and I couldn't believe the results, but I knew right then and there that I wanted to be a good mother. I loved my baby. I wanted to protect my child and I knew he or she was a gift and had a great purpose–a blessing, despite my choices and circumstances.

It was with this child that God would begin showing me the depths of the correlation of the love between a child and parent with that of us and God. That correlation was there my entire life through my relationship with my parents, especially Daddy. But now, it would take on a deeper meaning since I held the role of parent. My life was no longer about me but about my baby. *Is it a boy or a girl? What names do I have in mind? When is the perfect time to tell my parents? There isn't one.* I walked around with the weight of this news for what seemed like months even though it'd only been days. Days turned into a couple of weeks. I looked at people and decided if they would judge me or not once word got out. Here I was, a 20-year-old pregnant college student, unwed, and the bishop's daughter. What a headline this would be. So, I continued to carry it, alone.

Mom would talk to me and at times, it was like I couldn't hear what she was saying because my head was filled with thoughts of telling her. I just didn't have the courage because once I said something, "normal" would no longer be. I went to work, withdrew some at church, and already felt condemned, so I wondered what it would feel like once the cat was actually out of the bag.

I eventually started with my siblings. My sister and I recently discussed how I told her. Neither of us could remember. However, I vividly remember the experience I had with my brother. One evening, my brother randomly came up to me and put his hand, which looked as if it was holding something, up to my stomach. He proceeded to play around and say, "I'm giving you an ultrasound." I couldn't believe it. I looked at him soberly and told him I would be right back. I went upstairs to grab the paper I received from Planned Parenthood for confirmation. When I returned, I handed it to him. His eyes grew big and a surprised smile came across his face as he said, "I was just playing." We sat there for a few moments as he silently dealt with it and my heart raced but just a little. Suddenly he asked, "Have you told Mom and Dad?" I let him know I hadn't. He wanted me to let him know before I did so he could not be there when I did. We laugh about it now, but I understood him then. If I could not have been there when I told them, I wouldn't have. I knew that it would be the hardest thing, at that time, that I would go through.

On the afternoon of July 8th, I was at home in our living room. I could feel the fuzzy, soft, peach carpet underneath my feet as I sat in the brown, high-backed chair just to think. Deep in thought and not aware of what my face looked like, Mom came and sat next to me. My heart started that racing thing again. *Just act normal, Mariesa.* She inquired about what was going on and told me she noticed I hadn't been myself lately. Without warning, against my will, and out of a place of fear, a small flood of tears escaped my eyes and she knew, she just knew. She may have known before the tear shedding, but now, she *really* knew. My siblings wouldn't have told her; she had motherly discernment. She didn't say a word but just grabbed me and held me as I cried. She assured me that whatever it was, it would be okay. Even as I type, tears come to my eyes because I remember how I felt her unconditional, unadulterated love overwhelm me. She lightly rocked me and her first biological grandchild too.

After the tears though, it was time to talk, but I stayed silent. So Mom opened her mouth and asked, "Do you think you're pregnant?"

I replied, "I know I am."

The silence lingered for what felt like an eternity. She asked a few questions very calmly although I knew her heart may have kept up with mine then. We just had a heart-to-heart talk. I didn't feel condemned, thought of differently, or judged. I felt love, compassion, and still some nervousness. She said to me, "See, I'm not a monster." We chuckled ever so lightly and she smiled. I know she thought about how long I'd been carrying this news without her when she probably should have been the first person I went to. She was my mother, the very one who carried me and labored to get me into the world. She cared for me when I couldn't care for myself and even after I had learned. And at this time when I was faced with, or should I say getting ready to be faced with unimaginable scrutiny and possible discrimination, she was by my side, loving on, and reassuring me.

Amongst the hard conversation and loving on me, she announced that I had to tell my dad. The panic came rushing in a little heavier. One parent down, one to go, and Mom was the easier one. I didn't even tell her, she told me. Dad was already dealing with so much. How was I going to break his heart with the knowledge of my sin? No, my baby wasn't a sin, but the premarital sex was. Despite my sin though, God blessed me tremendously and I would come to know just how much as time went on.

Not long after, Mom and I went shopping for baby items. I have to admit, it was exciting. God entrusted me to bring new life into the world to further His Kingdom. What an honor; what a privilege. I just had to jump over a few more hurdles before it started to actually feel like what I knew it was. Mom asked me when I thought I was going to tell him. She and I thought about when it would be best. He'd been having really good days lately, and I didn't want to put a halt to them. Approaching, was a Sunday night church service in which Dad would have a special guest speaker. He was excited about the service and more so about the speaker. We concluded that I would tell him after that service. You know, let everything be normal for him until then.

That Sunday night, July 11th, the service was good, but I definitely couldn't enjoy it. I sat there with the thought of Dad's reaction at the forefront of my mind. *How will I say it? What will he say? What will he do?* It was positively the only thing I could think about and for sure one of the most frightening as well.

Upon getting home, it almost felt like I was having an out-of-body experience. I sat at the dining room table, occasionally glancing down the hall toward my parents' bedroom, dreading the next minutes. I continuously rehearsed words in my brain as nothing seemed to sound right. There was nothing right about that moment and the feeling that I felt. My stomach was in knots. You already know what my heart was doing. Mom sat down across from me at the table. She shared some of these same physical going-ons, I could tell. She asked, "Do you want me to tell him?" I told her "Thank you," but I would do it. I thought Mom telling him may have been worse. Once she told him, he would have sought me out, 'cause I probably would have tried to hide. I just thought it best that I tell him. I couldn't bear to listen in for his reaction or hear his footsteps coming toward me after he learned the news. So after quite a bit of time stalling, thinking, and analyzing, I got up with sweaty, pulsing palms, a heart that I just knew had a great chance of showing itself, and insides that were literally shaking, to walk what felt like the green mile down the hallway to tell Dad he was going to be a Paw Paw.

Jen

There I stood, looking at Dad as he comfortably lay in bed enjoying his show after having a wonderful night at church. That was where his wonderful night would end and my sin, in and of itself but also the blowback to come from it, would be the cause. I searched for the words to say and all I could come up with was, "Dad, I messed up."

As he looked at me, he asked, "Messed up, how?"

To which I replied, "With a guy."

I instantaneously saw the hurt in his eyes. Then he sat up and asked, "Are you pregnant?" I simply said, "Yes." The heaviness of my "yes" filled the room, and my out-of-body experience expired as I seemed to soak in that moment, not voluntarily though. Time seemed to stand still.

After my "yes," it's all a blur. It's taken me quite a while to pen these specific moments in my life. I remember saying yes, but after that, I had such trouble recollecting much else from that night. I didn't even journal about it. I've thought about why that may have been. All I could come up with is that it was due to the trauma of it all. Trauma? You may ask. Yes, trauma. My pregnancy and the gift of my baby were not traumatic. It was experiencing this almost paralyzing fear and feeling of condemnation (versus conviction previously felt before pregnancy occurred) behind confronting my dad with this information–that was traumatic. But only slightly because the trauma train was soon to mow me over with the next group of people I would be summoned to confess my sins to.

Before getting to that, I'd like to give some background information about the church my dad pastored that I was born in, grew up in, and attended well into adulthood. The church was founded in 1922 in the hills of Kentucky. One of the founders was my great, great, great aunt on my mother's side. After some years in Kentucky, my aunt and my uncle (her husband) relocated and began pastoring in Ohio in 1948. Starting in the 70s, my dad worked alongside her in the ministry for many years, which prepared him for the call on his life. My aunt continued to serve and lead the church faithfully until her illness prevented her from doing so. With prompting from God, my aunt made it known that Dad was to pastor the church. He began to lead the church shortly before her passing.

Before I go into further descriptions, I want to make it known that in no way is my intent to disparage the church. I am grateful for my home church because it is where I learned about God, had early experiences with Him, and it laid the foundation for who I am today. With that said, it was an old-fashioned holiness church. If you know anything about (some) holiness churches, you know that some of the people were very sincere and genuine in their pursuit of God and in pleasing Him. Because of this pursuit, there were very strict teachings in the church which led to strict lifestyles.

To give a few examples of the teachings, women were discouraged from wearing pants, makeup (including colored nail polish), and most jewelry (no earrings). Long skirts and stockings were what most of the women wore. Going to the movies and attending professional sporting events were also frowned upon. I don't think I saw my first movie in the theater until I was a teenager and that would've made both of my older siblings grown when they did so. A lot of our teenagers couldn't go to the prom or school dances because of the dancing and the worldly music. By the time my generation came along, Dad had liberated us from some of those things, but I almost didn't get to go to prom. I hadn't been to any homecomings or other dances, and I hadn't even considered going because I figured I wouldn't be allowed. But because I was president of my senior class, Dad let me go to prom. A list could be inserted here of rules and traditions that weren't necessary for a relationship with Jesus, however, my goal is not to spend a lot of time on this but rather paint a small picture of some of what I grew up under.

Lastly, some holiness churches' members including but not limited to the Mother's Board (seasoned women in the church), would get a bad rap as coming off mean, rude, or too forward when it came to rules and applying them to our lives. I just want to interject that although a few people were mean-spirited, there were plenty more who were some of the sweetest, loving, and godly people you would ever meet. Under Dad's leadership, further progress was made through knowledge and study of the scriptures which led to more understanding throughout the years. With that understanding and revelation, things loosened up some. None of which contradicted the Bible.

With all of that said, hopefully, you have a clearer understanding of why my "yes" to Dad asking if I was pregnant held so much weight. We both knew that one of the rules that hadn't been lifted from the church was confessing and apologizing for certain sins to and in front of the church congregation. Fornication was one of those sins which required a public apology to our local assembly. Once I did this, my good news would spread like wildfire but not as good news, as slanderous gossip–possibly destroying my reputation as "the bishop's daughter" along the way.

The bishop's daughter wasn't a title that I asked for, but it was one that came with Dad's leadership. It wasn't the essence of who I was–there's a difference between position and being. I was Mariesa–a somewhat soft-spoken young lady who loved God, loved her family, earned good grades in school, and mostly minded her own business. Along with that, I was super flawed, made a plethora of mistakes, and didn't understand the calling on my life or how this "role" I inherited was a whole preparation process to fulfilling the said calling. The times I had to bite my tongue so that my words and reaction wouldn't fall back on Dad's name, was such good practice for my actual purpose. I wasn't aware of it then and even though my feelings were valid, I had too much respect for my dad to turn my words loose. Even though it felt unfair that others could allow their unwarranted opinions out and freely say how they felt, I could not.

Walking in the space of the bishop's daughter/family was tough, but daily answering the call of the bishop was even tougher. The crazy thing is, it's people who make it tough, not the call itself. Yes, the call is not an easy road, it costs something. However, when people allow themselves to be influenced by Satan, pride, self-seeking agendas, and operating from a place opposite of love, come out. So, on top of already having that pressure, I was about to add fuel to the fire.

The days were numbered before I made my debut as an unwed pregnant woman. Dad and I talked quite a bit, against my will. It was more listening to him than me talking. I responded to a question; I wasn't trying to be disrespectful, but it was more than difficult to process everything. I was excited about the new life I carried, but at the same time, a little nervous to become a mother. I knew I could do it with God, but because of the guilt I carried as a result of my transgressions, I questioned if God was still with me. I resorted to partial solitude and withdrew myself a little more than usual those days.

Right after I found out I was pregnant, I "sat myself down" at church. Quite honestly, I should have done so before the pregnancy began. I don't know if it's possible to "sit *yourself* down," but I did–unofficially. If you're unfamiliar with the term "sat down," it's a discipline that happens in which the person is no longer allowed to function at church. For example, this person isn't permitted to sing in the choir, usher, or fulfill any other type of ministry role. The period for which a person is "sat down" varies and you see this discipline happen mostly with unwed women who are pregnant. I witnessed someone getting "sat down" once, not because she was the only one who sinned but because she was the one whose sins had proof. This young woman was one of my best friends that I spoke of earlier. Just a little over two years prior, I sat in the congregation and balled my eyes out when she, with a shaky voice, struggled through her tears while standing before the church to apologize. I wasn't crying because of her sin; that had long been over with. I cried *with* her because I could see the pain of shame and guilt in her at those moments. I felt so bad. I wondered why she couldn't just "sit down" and not have to beg the pardon of people who had all sinned and fallen short of the glory of God. I just wanted to grab and hold her close to remind her that she was forgiven and not condemned. I didn't like crying, but to see my friend like that made the tears I fought so hard to contain, gush out and down my face with such force. Unbeknownst to me at the time, I would stand before the congregation next.

Eleven

It was a warm Tuesday evening in mid-July of 2004. This Tuesday evening Bible study was no different from the rest except that it was–the parishioners just didn't know it yet. Bible study always started at 7:30 pm with a song and prayer. Not long after, the service would be turned over to Dad for him to teach the lesson. It was the most unnerving study I'd ever been in and the time seemed to drag by. I just wanted to get my apology over with, but the entire time, I kept thinking about what I would say. Again, I wanted to formulate my words just right. How do you do that though? I was a ball of nerves, as I sat there waiting as the Word of God was being taught. It's safe to say that I didn't take any of it in. All that I focused on was how much more my family and I would be a target for opinions, questions (asked and in peoples' heads), and whispers.

Before we went to church, I could sense a little bit of Dad's nervousness because he would ask if I was alright and maybe even if I was ready. At times, it appeared he was deep in thought. No, I wasn't ready for this but it was what "we the church" did. I couldn't say that to him, but what I did tell Dad was that I was more concerned about him and my family versus what could've possibly been said about me. I said something like, "As long as my family is okay, I don't care much about the opinions of others regarding me." Dad must've thought my remarks came from a prideful place because he corrected me and told me not to be like that. It didn't come from a place of arrogance or pride, it came from my "family comes first" mindset. I knew that if everyone else turned their backs on me, I could always count on my family; they would never turn their backs on me. Other than God Himself, the nucleus of my immediate family held me together. I wanted them to be okay.

I was aware of what I'd done. I was even okay with getting "sat down." I understood that I could no longer sing in the choir or on the praise team because of my actions. I knew that disciplinary action had to take place because I certainly didn't want to be a stumbling block for anyone or be the reason why someone didn't come to church. The part that I didn't agree with, and it didn't matter if I agreed with any of it or not, was standing before and repenting to the people. At times, I thought to myself, *If asking for forgiveness from congregations when one sinned wasn't exclusive to premarital sex with proof (pregnancy), every single person would be humiliated in the same way.*

I believe I drove myself to church that evening, and I had a bag packed. I planned to stay at my sister's that night to lay low and not be around if the house phone was to start ringing after church. I was trying to protect myself from hearing what could possibly come. I put up a wall to guard my mind and my heart.

I sat next to or close to my mom because I truly needed to breathe her in, during these moments. While I squirmed in my seat, I occasionally glanced around the sanctuary and thought, *They have no idea what's about to happen.* I even made mental notes of one of the routes the news would take. It was really about to spread like wildfire in the driest of forests. I was about to light the match when I told the news and then drop it when I walked away from the microphone.

Eventually, it was time. Time moved slowly, but I couldn't stop it altogether. No matter what, the clock kept ticking and the time would come. It *had* come, and Dad called me up to stand before a curious congregation. I stood up, matches in hand, and put one foot in front of the other while empathizing with Hester Prynne, from *The Scarlet Letter*, along the way. Once I reached my dad, standing there on the altar, I stood behind the microphone. The last thing I'd uttered in the microphone was praises to God through song quite a while before that night. This time, it was different. There would be no praises but rather a confession flowing from my lips. No tears were surfacing from my eyes. After rehearsing the words several times, the same type of shaking voice I heard from my best friend came trembling out of me. Still no tears. I simply said (partially paraphrased due to lack of recollection). "I never thought I would have to stand before you to do this, but I stand here to ask for your forgiveness." Match lit. I didn't say much else but for sure a little more of which has escaped me now. I was just completely humiliated and wanted to go back and not sit down, but sink into the pew next to my mom. I couldn't even say that I was pregnant and that was the reason I was up there asking for *their* forgiveness. So I walked back to my seat, the lit match still in hand. There was a little stirring in the congregation when all of a sudden, Dad said, "Mariesa didn't tell it all. SHE'S PREGNANT." Match. Dropped.

Like a perfectly timed chorus, I heard the collective gasp of the congregation. It was then that I felt like the scarlet *A* had been tattooed on my shirt. I sat there, eyes straight ahead, attempting to tune out the low rumble in the midst. My heart...you already know what it was doing. I was not looking forward to the benediction and dismissal, which would come shortly after, because that meant I would have to get up from the place I felt permanently glued to and walk down the aisle to get out the door. I thought about leaving early, you know, just slipping out the door real quick to get in my car and drive away. But I couldn't do that because, at some point, I would have to face the people. Why prolong what was already coming? When I say "face the people," I don't mean it like they were going to reprimand me, I'd already dealt with enough of that within myself. I simply mean to converse about it at all or get the looks from others. They may not have been negative looks, but I just wanted to leave and do so as quickly as possible.

After the final amen, people began to approach me most lovingly. Some of them had tears in their eyes and hugged me. I never figured out the reason for some of their tears. Were they disappointed in me, did they feel the same way I did when I watched my best friend do this, or what? Did they have sins to confess also? I guess it didn't matter because I felt love in those hugs and kisses. My church family (most of them) wrapped their loving arms around me, encouraged me, and supported me. They did what the church was supposed to do. Not everyone embraced me and gave me encouraging words, but I was so grateful for the ones who took the time to do so. I chose to focus on them. That *A* on my shirt began to fade a little because of their love.

I knew the "not the bishop's daughter" comments were coming, whether or not they reached me didn't matter–they were thought and said. Even if they didn't come from our local congregation, they were coming forth regardless–it was nothing new. For years, my sister and I (my brother also but in different words) endured the "and you're supposed to be the bishop's daughter" or the "I'm gon' tell yo' daddy" remarks from people in our organization. It was over the most stupid things too. But *that* time, I guess I'd given them something to really talk about.

When I got to my sister's that night, my best friend called me to find out where I was and then she came to me because she had heard. I hadn't told her beforehand. As I said, I withdrew myself from just about everyone. We sat and talked for quite a while; it made my heart glad that once she found out, she came to be with me. She knew what I was feeling. That whole thing helped us bond on a new level. We joked and laughed some, it got my mind off of a lot of it.

That same night, Dad called my phone to check on me. I let him know that I was okay. I hoped he and Mom were too, but I just had to take a little time away. The hard part was now over and I could begin living my life again, just differently and with more than normal commentary surrounding me. Some of it got back to me, but I'm sure most of it didn't. Either way, I had no time to focus on the people around me. My focus was on the one growing inside me.

Twelve

The remainder of the summer consisted of me working at the portrait studio, preparing for my second, full year of college, and preparing for my baby. My parents made it crystal clear that they didn't want me to move out. They were steadfast about me staying at home so they could help me with the baby and so I would have the support I needed. I was so grateful for their love. It reflected God's love for his children. Through falling short, living with the illusion of control, and making poor choices, God still loves us and longs for us to stay close to Him. He desires for us to abide in Him no matter how many times we have messed up, how far we've strayed, or how low people's opinions of us are. His love is unmatched.

I kept going to church and sitting in the audience. After service one day, my godfather approached me, looking pretty bothered by something. He told me that when he scanned the crowd from the pulpit during service, I looked down or sad. He let it be known that he didn't like that. While encouraging me to keep my head up and not be sad, he reminded me that I didn't have a reason to hold my head down. I always remembered and appreciated it even as I became older and time went on. Dad saw the conversation happening from a distance, so when we arrived home, he inquired.

He, too, was appreciative of my godfather's words. Dad told me that God had already forgiven me, so I needed to forgive myself.

In the fall, I found out I was having a baby boy. I was ecstatic because I always wanted to have a boy first. I imagined the bond my son and I would have. I made sure I ate healthy meals, eliminating things I loved to eat and replacing them with healthier options to make sure I did my part to help my baby grow healthy. The excitement settled in because my mom, sister, and I began shopping more for him.

It seemed like I was always good with children. I loved babies. It was like they gravitated towards me or I towards them. For years before this, children at the church would even come to sit with me during service. Mom and I babysat for a close friend of the family when I was a preteen/fresh teen. We kept two children overnight, one of which was a baby girl, while their mother worked. One day, I held the baby girl in my arms when she was close to one year old. As I held her, I told her how successful she would be, how loved she was, how God loved her, and so on. At the time, I didn't even know what I was doing, but now, as a mother of four, I realize I was speaking life over that baby. When I spoke to her, she locked eyes with me and stopped moving. She laid in my arms ever so attentively and seemed to absorb everything I was saying. I was sure she didn't understand me; she was too young. Looking back, I know that the Spirit of God was there with us and He was ministering to her through me. It was a powerful moment. I felt the power at the moment but didn't fully understand it. I was just the vessel. When I felt led, I began to do this with other children and babies who I had the privilege of watching or spending time with. I would continue with my own children as God blessed me each time they arrived on the scene of my life.

Even though I had been around several babies and children, I was never a mother until now. There was much I needed to learn, so I continually expanded my knowledge about pregnancy, birth, and babies. One thing I noticed while I sat in class one day was that my teeth hurt. I'd never experienced tooth pain like that. When I spoke with a nurse in my midwife's office, I was informed that when the baby isn't getting enough calcium, the first place they'll pull it from is the mother's teeth. To provide my son with what he needed, the need would be pulled from his source of life while in my womb. Sheesh! I was shocked. So when this happened again, I would leave class, drink a bunch of milk, and the pain would subside. I found it quite interesting; I was just amazed at the human body and how God designed it to do things we will never fully know. To avoid the need to down milk like that, I began to take calcium supplements along with my prenatal vitamins. That was a game changer and my teeth felt so much better afterward.

One cool Sunday morning, I was in bed and I felt this little flutter in my stomach. I didn't think too much of it at first, possibly thinking it was just a sign of hunger or something. Then it occurred to me that I had just felt, for the first time, my baby boy moving inside me. I knew he'd been moving the whole time, but now what was growing on the inside, could not only be visible on the outside but felt too. I called Mom into my room and she came right in. I laid still so that the flutter would come back, then I placed her hand on my stomach and told her what I'd just felt. We waited as the movement–further evidence of this miracle–excited us.

Just as there were visible outward signs of life happening on the inside of me, there were visible outward signs of what was happening on the inside of my dad's body. He became tired quicker and more often. Even though it didn't look good, we knew God was able to speak a word and everything could change. I noticed him shaving one day. He struggled as his hand was weak and his grip on the razor wasn't strong. As he trembled, he nicked himself. Watching this brought on an overwhelming sense of sadness. At the same time, I wanted to help him as much as I could. I told him I would shave him, but he was determined to use his hand.

As we played Uno, he could barely pick a card off the deck with his dominant hand. I saw his frustration, so I started to hand him cards when needed. Even though the decline was evident in much of what he did, I wanted to make normal for him what I could. So I didn't stop making him draw two or draw four. And with a smirk on my face, I drew the cards for him and handed them to him. He would say, "I see how you do me." Dad had a way of making you laugh. He was fun, even through this.

On a cool, crisp, autumn Sunday afternoon in November of 2004, Dad called our family into his church office after service. The church was cleared of members, as they all went to their respective places. As I made my way through the empty sanctuary and the door situated in the far left corner next to the stage, I wondered what was going on. As we–Dad, Mom, my brother, my sister, and I–gathered in the cozy office, I learned that Dad, not long prior, asked the doctor about his prognosis. We were about to find out what it was. Now before I proceed, I just have to give it up for my daddy. I watched him this whole time, not just at church but everywhere. I didn't even know he had gone to the doctor and received the news I'm about to share with you until that cool, autumn day I speak of. As I was saying, the doctor told Dad, "It's gonna get cha." Like that was it. There was nothing else the doctor felt could be done. Dad was given approximately one year to live. I was shocked. Close to five years after his diagnosis, we sat with this heavy prognosis. *One year. How? After all the treatments–the surgery, the hormone therapy, the chemotherapy, the radiation, the liquid chemotherapy, and the blood transfusions. Why were we at this point?* It was such a tough pill to swallow. There were tears shed. One thing my family never did was sit around and cry–that was new. That day, we wept together. Our tears seemed to bond us together even closer as the pain penetrated each of us individually.

We were (are) an extremely tight-knit family and it would be no different afterward. Dad stood up and had us stand with him. He took us under his arms and somehow managed to hold us all at the same time, together. We stood there in his quaint office, holding each other. Through the tears and with great strength, Dad told us that he didn't want us to go down in sackcloth and ashes. It was understandable because who wants to go through illness in their body and be reminded of what they are faced with when looking at those around you? He told us that dying was easy, it was the suffering that was hard and he didn't care to go through it. Then he made one of the most profound declarations. I distinctly remember it and can almost hear him say it. He said, "This is why I've been living right." Even though I was emotional, Dad's words brought a sense of calm to the storm. At that moment, God's strength was evident through Dad, and that same strength would carry us through. We knew that when a doctor gave a prognosis, even the doctor would not know for sure. We knew that God had the final answer and in Him, we placed our faith.

When walking out of the office, I felt emptier than the quiet sanctuary. You know when devastating things happen in life, it's like it's hard to focus on much else. Even if your mind isn't thinking about the devastating thing, it is always in the back of your mind.

The thing often resurfaces to steal your joy, it seems.

One evening not long after our family meeting, I found myself in my thoughts again. Dad's prognosis was fresh in my mind. I thought about his words. The dying may not have been what bothered him, but it sure bothered me. It may have been easy for him, but not for me. Not for us. I knew he wanted to be with us and may not have wanted to leave us, but I understood his point. I comprehended that suffering was undesirable. The pain and agony were what I imagined back in 1999 when I learned that this disease had come into our lives on a very personal level. I had already seen so much but knew that the worst was still to come. It would be the worst, then the best, for him. The house was quiet, but my thoughts were so loud. They would not shut up or turn off. All of a sudden, I heard Dad's voice. I hadn't even noticed his presence. He said, "You're not lying around all sad, are you?" A little startled, I looked his way, gave him a small smile, and told him I was okay. Then he wanted to talk. He said, "You know I probably won't be here to see you graduate college." I shook my head to acknowledge that I understood. He proceeded, "I want you to promise me that you will finish school." With a hurting but determined heart, I gave him my word.

Dad's suffering became more intense as time went on. His energy depleted quicker and he grew weaker. One day, I was home alone and I saw Dad drive in front of our house and pull into our driveway. He usually parked his car in our detached, two-car garage in the space furthest from the house. A walkway went from our driveway, up between the house and garage, and to the side porch. I knew that once Dad got out of the car, it wouldn't take him long to come inside the house. I waited for a while to hear his key in the door but never did. Growing concerned, I looked out the window to see if, perhaps, he was talking with a neighbor or something on his way into the house, but he wasn't. I didn't see him at all. After approximately 20 minutes (give or take a few), my mind raced with possibilities. My heart raced as thoughts of going out to the garage and finding that he had transitioned, wouldn't leave my head. Mom would not be home from work for a while, and if he was hurting or needed help, I didn't want him suffering and without assistance. Then if Mom came home and Dad had gone to be with Jesus, I didn't want her to find him out there. There was no one home but me, so I prayed, put my shoes on, and headed to the side door to see about him. When I opened the door and looked down the walkway, there was my daddy on the ground. He was on his hands and knees trying to crawl up the walkway to get into the house. My heart sank. I wasn't sure what had happened, but I yelled, "Daddy!" I rushed to his side. Panting for breath, Dad tried to explain that he just didn't have any energy. I felt helpless. It was cold out there, his black, leather jacket wasn't zipped and his leather hat surely couldn't have kept his head warm. The ground was frigid and here Dad was struggling to muster up the energy to crawl across it to reach warmth in the house. I couldn't pick him up and he didn't want me to. He told me to get out of the cold. So, I went and stood in the doorway to watch this heart-wrenching scene play out before my eyes. The ability to crawl seemed to have escaped him as he struggled to move his hands and knees. Little by little and with many breaks, Dad made it to the bottom of the porch steps; I did my best to encourage him along the way. "Just a little more Dad. You're almost here." I'm not sure if it was annoying to him or not, but he made it to me. Then it was a battle to crawl up the stairs, another very slow process. I held the door as he pulled himself across the floor of the landing that he had once had the energy to paint light blue. There was a step up from the landing that brought you into the dining room. Once inside the house and across the landing, Dad sat on the edge of the step just at the beginning of the dining room. He sat and rested there on the soft, fuzzy, peach carpet while leaning his exhausted body against the off-white wall. I sat with him. He closed his eyes and tried to catch his breath for a few minutes. In my mind, I prayed for guidance on how to help him get to his bedroom in the back of the house. When he regained just enough strength, I assisted him in standing up. He stood there, leaning over the dining room chair closest to him. His eyes darted around to see what he could grab to help support him to take his next steps. The TV stand was his next anchor, then it was the counter. He ploddingly made his way to the stove and while leaning on it, tried to figure out how he would make it down the hallway because there was nothing for him to hold or lean on. The whole time, he tried talking to me as his breathing was slightly labored. Much of the time, his eyes were closed as his body screamed for rest. I quickly grabbed the stool in the kitchen while he leaned against the stove. The stool had a back to it and would be stable enough for him to hold onto and even lean against as needed. He had a cane somewhere in the house, but at that point, it wouldn't help him. I told him that I would put the stool in front of him and he could hold it while walking up to it. I told him to take his time and as he was ready, I would move the stool back some more. We would repeat this process until we reached his room. I was in no rush, I just wanted him to be okay. We inched down the hallway, little by little. With each step, it looked like there was more and more effort behind it. We eventually made it to his bed. I knelt, took his shoes and socks off, helped him get into something more comfortable, cleaned his hands, picked his legs up, and put them in the bed as he lay on his side. I finally covered him up with the sheet and blanket, placing it over his ear, down his jawline, and under his chin. I don't know what it was about the cover over the ear, but I knew it would be comforting to him, as this is something we both did.

When Mom got home from work, I filled her in on the whole ordeal. His illness was taking more of a toll on him and he needed to have more help during the day. Mom came off of her job temporarily to help Dad as he was no longer able to do some things without assistance. Her last day of work was on December 17, 2004.

The very next day, Dad was crippled by the pain. At this point, there had been many times when Mom would have me get my brother to come and pray for Dad while she stayed by his side, especially during the night. It was all too familiar to be awakened by the sound of my dad in agonizing pain. To hear him cry out, was and still is unexplainable. When that piercing sound would penetrate my eardrums, I would lay as still as I could and cry with him. I would pray for God to touch his body so he wouldn't have to suffer so much. That day was no different. As evening approached, I prayed silently within myself. His pain became so bad that I drove him, accompanied by Mom, to the hospital. Once we got there, he sat in the wheelchair until they admitted him. Sporadically, he would wince up and just groan.

The same day, we had our church winter recreation. I looked forward to the recreations each year because our church family would come together, have food, play organized games, and have a really good time together. This year was so different. I sat at the foot of the hospital bed once he was admitted and all settled in. He told me to go to the recreation, so I did. It was so hard to see him in pain and not be able to do anything for him. It seemed like he was having more bad than good days then–it was either pain, low energy, nausea, or several other complications and side effects.

The pain patches were no longer sufficient. The insufficiency landed him in the hospital several times, but this time, his doctor took it up a notch. Dad began receiving stronger pain medication through his port, located in his left arm. He would now have to carry a pain pump with him to ensure the continuous intravenous flow of relief to his body. After a few days, Dad was released from the hospital. The increase in pain indicated the spread of his cancer; it was aggressive. It metastasized to other areas of his body, including his bones. As a result, Dad grew weaker.

Christmas Day was sad. Our family would usually have breakfast, family prayer, and then sit in the living room to open presents together. This year was so different. Dad was tired and weak. He wasn't able to come out to partake in our usual family traditions, so I brought the present I'd gotten him to his bedside. He couldn't get down the stairs to his office in the basement, so I gifted him a lap desk in hopes it would aid him in his studies or whatever he chose to do on it. Of course, it was meant to be temporary, just until he could go up and down the stairs again. He thanked me and we had one of our meaningful talks while he lay there in his bed.

Tasks that we often took for granted when we completed them, now became more taxing. One day, I heard a thud and Mom yelling in panic. Dad had fallen out of the shower and said he had lost his balance. Some of my memory is a little foggy, but I remember it was a struggle to get Dad up again. I was pregnant and not much help when it came to lifting people or things, mostly because they wouldn't let me.

One bitterly cold afternoon, Mom took Dad to his doctor's office. There was hard snow and ice on the ground. Dad, still using his legs, was determined to do everything he could while he still could. Once I saw them arrive back home, I opened the side door. I waited, there on the landing, until I saw them coming up the walkway and closer to the porch stairs. I opened the screen door and held it so that Mom and I could easily get Dad in. I watched as he took a step up on the first stair. He slowly put his foot on the second stair and I sensed he would fall. While attempting to step up, Dad fell backward, taking Mom out with him. Mom didn't fall completely, but Dad did. He lay there on the snow and ice, in pain and trying to gather himself to get up. Tears welled up in my eyes. Mom looked so sad. Dad seemed to try to keep his brave face on, but I knew he was cold and hurting. Somehow gaining his bearings and with help from Mom, he got up and made it into the house.

A little later, while he was in bed, a beeping noise was heard every now and again. The noise alerted him and panic set in as he thought something may have been damaged on his pain pump from the impact of his fall. The medicine had not long ago been changed, and we checked it. The bag was still intact and no indicators of anything being wrong were shown on the screen. Dad heard the beeping noise again and called us into the room. He knew that if he weren't getting an adequate amount of morphine, the pain would come back and grip him fiercely. The look on his face was sheer apprehension. We did our due diligence in making sure the pump was working, the batteries were fresh, and nothing was wrong. The screen still showed that everything was functioning fine and his medicine would not stop or be delayed. But the beeping noise occurred again minutes later. Dad grew more concerned as the anticipation of the pain filled his mind. Listening for the beep again, we stayed in the area and once we heard it, I got down on the floor because that is where the noise seemed to come from. Surprisingly, I saw Dad's cell phone lying just under the bed. I picked it up and saw that his battery was low. The phone was where the noise came from. Once Dad heard and saw the phone, he was overcome with gladness. His whole demeanor changed from worry to relief.

If uncontrolled, the pain would have overtaken Dad. I was grateful for the medication that kept the pain from being felt. From the looks of things, Dad's physical pain would soon transfer to the pain of losing him. I was not ready for that. I also was not ready to watch him suffer, but there we were. Even though Dad was not bothered by death, I was. I had never seen it so up close and personal. I watched as it slowly but steadily ran its course until it picked up the pace. Dad began to walk more with a cane as the strength in his legs decreased.

One of his last services at church was on a Sunday morning in either January or early February. He was carried up the stairs in a wheelchair by some of the men of the church. He was then wheeled up to the front. I don't believe Dad was there the entire service, but toward the end, he addressed the congregation. Even though his legs were not as steady as they once were, Dad carefully stood up, took his cane, and with my mother under his arm helping him, he walked slowly across the front of the sanctuary in praise to God. Then he walked back to his wheelchair. The congregation clapped and praised God with him as they looked on. He yelled out, "Hallelujah," with a voice that wasn't as strong as it once was.

Dad was a praiser. In chapter two, I wrote about when we were in the mall after his surgery and he bellowed out with praise. That was just one of the times he burst out with thanksgiving to God. There are so many more instances that I could write about, but one, in particular, happened several weeks before this day at church.

I went out to eat with Mom, Dad, and two other couples (my parent's friends) from the church. There was a restaurant that Dad took my family to when I was little and it quickly became one of our favorites. It was about 30 minutes away and Dad drove us all there, in my mom's minivan. While we ate, Dad started praising God loudly right in the restaurant. Tears came to his eyes as God's goodness overwhelmed him. Thankfulness poured out of his heart and onto his lips. He was so grateful to have a good day. Looking on, you wouldn't have known that he was so sick. Others joined in with him in praise but a lot quieter. I watched him and I will always remember that Dad gave God praise through it all.

There were times while he was driving (throughout my life) that he would raise his hand and pray in tongues. I didn't always understand his loud and sporadic praise and what seemed to be random prayer times, but I would come to understand it more and more as time went on. Even through Dad's suffering, God never changed. He was still faithful. He was still a healer. He was still God. We held onto the fact that at any time, God could speak a word and Dad would be completely healed and restored as if it never happened.

Thirteen

My due date was in February of 2005, and it was quickly approaching. The baby's room was painted just how I wanted it. I always loved Mickey Mouse, so that was the theme of the nursery. My mom and sister put together a wonderful baby shower for me and the baby. There was so much love and so many gifts showered upon us. After the shower, friends helped us get everything into the house. In time, my sister and I organized everything. He had so many clothes, diapers and wipes galore, and just about everything that I needed or wanted. I always wanted to have a glider chair so that I could sit and rock him. I was able to purchase one with monetary gifts and gift cards. We were so blessed to have such support. I realized there was a time when having a baby shower was frowned upon if you were an unwed mother [in the church]. The thing is, the baby is coming and will need things regardless of one's personal feelings. I've heard it said, that it may seem like sex before marriage was condoned and encouraged if love and support were shown via a baby shower. I never understood that, but I'm so grateful that the women and those around me were there to help and love me. It was definitely what I needed, especially during such a time of transition. New life was beginning, but at the same time, a life that brought me forth seemed to be ending.

When I purchased the glider chair and it was assembled in the baby's room, my mom and I helped Dad walk down the hall to the nursery. Once inside, he looked around at all the baby's clothes hung up so neatly in the closet. An abundance of diapers and wipes, along with all the gifts, caused Dad to become overwhelmed–the good kind of overwhelmed. He sat in the newly put-together glider and could hardly believe his eyes. I also believe he thought about how he may never have the chance to rock his grandson in that chair.

During those days, Dad did a lot of thinking. His life had completely changed from the one he had known for decades before. It changed from a life of independence to reliance upon others to help him. I don't think he particularly cared for that, but it was necessary, and he was a good patient. Some of the time, I would catch him in thought and occasionally ask him what was on his mind. One memory that probably will never leave the file cabinet of my mind is the time Dad was sitting in his recliner in the living room and I sat on the sofa across from him. He began to express how he knew God could speak a word that would cause him to be healed. With tears in his eyes, he said (paraphrased), "I know God can do it, but I don't understand why He won't." That did something to me. We all knew God was able, but bowing to His will and His sovereignty was hard for me. I also understood that Dad had lots of strong medication constantly pumping through his body and at various times, he hallucinated, talked in his sleep, and had waves of emotions, among other various side effects. I also recognized that Dad was tired. His body endured so much up to that day and what he was going through was a result of sin entering the world–it just didn't sit right with him. Tearful, my heart broke as he uttered those words.

Days later, Dad called me into his room to talk. He told me not to let what he did or said, shake my faith. I figured he'd given additional thought to his words and maybe my reaction to them. I appreciated him telling me that, but I knew he was human. He didn't need to put on a brave face for me; he had always been and forever would be my hero. In those times of vulnerability, I felt closer to Dad. Those were precious moments of intimacy and relatability. He didn't seem weak or flawed but rather strong and courageous to even express his feelings. I respected his realness because it would help me in those times I may have ever questioned God about why. His vulnerability helped me to also be vulnerable and transparent to help others.

Toward the end of January, Dad's ability to walk was completely gone. Before, he could go out to the living room and sit in his recliner and even go to the bathroom on his own. At that point, he couldn't do much of anything without someone either carrying him or assisting him from point A to point B. When someone loses their ability to walk, there are so many factors that come into play that are rarely considered before it becomes a reality. I'll spare you most of the details, but it was a huge transition that we could see coming if God didn't intervene with healing on this side of heaven. Various times, Dad called me into his room to anoint him with oil and pray for his mind. He knew his body was declining quickly, but he also knew the battle was in his mind. Satan's attempts to tempt Dad would not go away just because he was sick and near death. Knowing that, he would pray and have us pray too. I was a little shy praying for him, in front of him, and at times, I would anoint him and pray quietly or in my mind. A time or two, I would lay hands on him just like he showed me when I was growing up. The difference though was that I wasn't touching his arm, back, or shoulder to pray for someone else with him, I was laying hands on the one who taught me to pray. I'd never considered that one day I would have to do this. When I dealt with sickness as a child, Dad would come to my bedside and pray for me. I knew that if he laid his hands on me, I would be okay. Then, it was my turn to stand at his bedside while he was ill to pray for him. I just hoped he would be okay.

So much was offered up on Dad's behalf. Churches held corporate prayers and fasts and individuals did the same thing. Many visitors came to visit and pray for Dad too. Love was shown through food, baked goods, and fruit basket deliveries. I can't begin to name all of the ways people gave to our family via time, talent, or treasure, but the best thing was prayer.

I fell asleep one night and God gave me a dream of comfort. In the dream, we (family and church family) were in a large hallway. The hallway floor consisted of low-cut carpet with a design on it (something like you might see on a hotel hallway floor), and extremely high ceilings that almost seemed non-existent because of their height and massiveness. In this hallway, we held hands in a circle. We prayed and praised God for Dad's healing. It was loud because of the singing, praying, and utterings. In the middle or inside the circle, was Dad. On the outside of the circle was an angel. The angel tried to get to Dad, but we kept blocking his way and continued to pray and praise. Finally, the angel stretched out his arm and just grabbed Dad gently. As the angel grabbed a hold of him, the pair started making their way out of and away from the circle. I yelled out, "Dad, wait! You can't walk!" Dad turned around and looked at me and said, "It's alright. I can walk now." He and the angel started walking and then running down the hallway. As they ran, they ascended to heaven.

That dream was one of the most powerful dreams that God had given me at that time. It was one in which God comforted me that Dad was going to be okay, healed even. As we stood around and prayed for Dad's healing, we were anticipating and expecting God to heal him on earth. Instead of receiving a temporary healing, he experienced and received a permanent healing–the ultimate healing.

I knew it was a matter of time before Dad's healing through transition would possibly take place. The signs were there–he wasn't eating much food. One day, Mom left the house to either grocery shop or get a small break from caregiving. My brother and I were there with Dad. He had some oatmeal he was supposed to eat and didn't want it. He had me mix in more milk to make it runny. Dad sat up on the side of the bed, legs dangling to the ground, with that bowl of oatmeal resting on a TV tray in front of him. Little by little, he ate it. He wanted to make sure I told Mom when she returned because it was a big accomplishment for him. I just smiled and told him I would let her know. He used to love Pepsi just like his mom did, I mean love it. He would drink it with his breakfast, lunch, dinner, and dessert. I can't even count the number of times I filled his cup with ice and poured it over the cubes. As the ice cracked and popped, fizz would rise to the top. I'd wait until it went down to continue filling the cup, close to the brim. As I walked down the hall, I always took a small sip. When I reached his room to sit it on his TV tray, he would ask, "Did you knock the poison off?" Most of the time, I replied, "Yup." But at this point, he wasn't even asking for nor drinking Pepsi and hadn't for quite some time.

Dad asked me if I wanted him to be there (still living) when I had the baby. It wasn't really a question though because he knew the answer. It was like a statement and he was hoping that it would be the case, if that makes sense. I answered anyway to make sure he was certain that I, for sure, wanted and needed him to still be with us when I gave birth to his grandson. His not being there at that time wasn't even something that crossed my mind. I'm sure Dad prayed for God to allow him a little while longer. In my mind, I had not considered that as long as he was still with us, he was not in the heavenly presence of God, and he would suffer. I just wanted my Daddy with me. I desired so strongly for him to meet my baby, his namesake.

My due date arrived. It was on a Sunday and I stayed home with Dad so my Mom could go to church with my brother. Later that afternoon, we were due at an out-of-town church for the pastor's appreciation service. So the plan was for me to stay home during our local morning service, then I would accompany my brother and our congregation out of town that afternoon for the second service. I laid there next to Dad, watching TV and talking a little. A lot of the time, he slept. I caught myself dozing off here and there too.

When I was a little girl, I would lie in bed with Dad and watch TV. Sometimes, we'd watch game shows–we were both pretty competitive when it came to games. Other times, or should I say most times, the TV would have "Murder She Wrote," "Matlock," or a sports game on it. If it was evening or nighttime, I'd stay there with him as long as I could to avoid going to bed. Eventually, Mom would come into the room and tell me it was bedtime because she wanted to lay down on her side and I occupied it. Many times, Dad would say to me, "Come on this side." With a huge smile on my face, I'd go over and lay on the little sliver of bed between Dad and the edge with such contentment. He would wrap one arm around me and the other he would prop his head up with either under his pillow. We continued to watch the show. The security I felt there with Daddy is indescribable. He was my safe place. After God, my first love. After a while of laying there, I'd get tired and try to keep my eyes open, but sleep would win every time. All of sudden, Dad would wake me when he asked, "Mese, are you sleeping?" I'd open my eyes as quickly as I could and say, "No." I wanted to stay there with him, in my safe place. He'd tell me to go to bed and I was obedient. Once I entered my room and lay in my bed, I was at peace and could fall asleep quicker than if I hadn't had that time with Dad.

Even though the circumstances changed quite a bit since those days, it still felt good to lay there next to Dad. He couldn't wrap his arm around me like he used to and barely kept his eyes open to watch TV, but to be in his presence still brought a security that only dads could bring. Here and there, he mumbled something in his sleep. The medicine had that effect on him.

After church, Mom and my brother came home and I got ready to go. It was very cold outside, so I dressed warmly. The afternoon service was just what I needed. It took my mind off of Dad a little and put my focus on God. The praises went forth to God in such a way that many danced before Him. No matter what went on in our lives, God never changed. He has always been and will always be the same. I remember praising God so hard that before I knew it, I was out in the aisle dancing before Him too. Need I remind you that it was my due date? I was a whole 40 weeks pregnant moving like I wasn't. I was careful, but I had to express myself to my God. At that point and for a little while before, I didn't care what people thought about me or what things got back to me that were said, praising Him would be the way I would get through that trying and transitional time in life.

Fourteen

That night after church, I laid in my bed wondering when my baby boy was going to grace us with his presence. I was a little sad because my due date had come and gone, and there were no signs of labor at all. I felt like I would be pregnant forever. I fell asleep, just a little while, and woke up for some reason. I thought to myself, *What if my water would break right now?* As I rolled from one side to the other, I felt a small gush of water and I couldn't believe it. I laid there for a little while longer to process everything and to test it. Sure enough, it was time. I got up and went to my parent's room quietly to not disturb Dad if he was asleep. I told Mom what had happened and she jumped up to help me. We woke my brother and I called my sister. Dad heard us whispering and asked if it was time, so we turned the lights on and started making the necessary moves. In the midst of what was a dark time for our family with death lingering near, there was a buzz of excitement and hope for the new life that would soon appear. I made other calls to my midwife and others. I was instructed to take my time getting to the hospital because it was my first baby and sometimes first babies take their time making their grand entrance into the world. I showered and ate graham crackers with peanut butter spread on them with a side of cinnamon applesauce. It was quite the combination, but I found myself eating it for a snack those days. My sister recorded a video to document the day. My family and I sat around and talked for a while, but then I started feeling little contractions. They prompted me to go to the hospital. One of my fears was that I would get sent back home because of false labor. I wasn't sure what I would experience other than pain and then joy after his arrival, but I knew that we were covered in prayer. As always, Dad prayed for me, and the baby, and for a smooth delivery before we left.

While in triage at the hospital, I was informed that I had a pinhole leak in my bag of water and it afforded me admission. I was super relieved to not go back home and glad I hadn't, ya know, on myself too. Once I was wheeled into my room with instructions on what to do, I went into the bathroom to put the hospital gown on. While I was there, I looked at myself in the mirror. As I stared in disbelief that it was happening, I took in all I had endured in my body to get to this point and all I'd pushed through mentally to bring my son into the world safely. I was excited, nervous, and afraid all at the same time. I knew for over nine months that he was preparing to be delivered, but there was no more preparation time, he was ready!

One of the questions the nurse asked me was if I wanted an epidural. Because I was afraid of the pain to come and because I'd witnessed labor that took days, I told her I thought I wanted one, but I wasn't 100 percent sure. Long story short, I ended up getting one at the appropriate time. I knew my body was capable of delivering my baby without medication, but because of what I had heard, I opted to numb the pain of the process.

A little later that same morning, I welcomed my son following the smooth delivery. It was a very short labor and my baby boy was healthy.

He was so beautiful; my heart was completely grateful. We were surrounded by so much love and support the entire time. Dad wasn't well enough to come to the hospital, of course, but I know he interceded in prayer for us at home. Either that morning I left to go to the hospital to deliver or days before, he asked if the hospital staff could possibly put a bed for him next to my bed so he could be there for me. Then he said it might be too much work for someone to carry him and put him in the car, unload him, and so on. Dad was trying to figure out how he could stay by my side and it meant the world to me. At the same time, it broke my heart. That was the beginning of me not having my dad for pivotal, life-changing, or even everyday moments. It was a little sobering. I wanted him to be at peace about not being able to go to the hospital. I let him know that it was okay and that I would call him. If he were well, I knew he would be there, without a doubt.

I don't know how many family members and friends were in and out of my room in support during and after labor, but I do know they showed up and showed out, in a great way. After a two-night hospital stay, we were discharged. The ride home felt so weird because the world seemed so much faster. I wanted to protect my baby from the world he was born into. He was so little and innocent. My whole world changed when my baby, who relied on me for everything, came into it. I anticipated getting home so I could introduce my son to my dad. Uncertain about how long they would have together, my goal was to get home so their time together could begin.

My sister and I pulled up to the house with precious cargo and as she got out, she video recorded as I took the car seat out of her car. My brother came outside to help us. He told Dad we were on the way home, so Dad started straightening the covers and sheets as much as he could. Mom and Dad's bed was one of the adjustable ones, so most of the day, Dad was sitting up in bed. He made sure his shirt was in place and that he looked okay. He anticipated the coming moments. It was a bright, sunny day. The white, fluffy clouds were beautiful with a vibrant blue sky in their background. I walked over a part of our front yard that had been somewhat destroyed with deep, muddy tire marks. They had been made from cars backing straight up to our front door to get Dad into the car for doctor's appointments, blood transfusions, etc. After finally getting in the house, I told my siblings I was so glad to be home. I took my newborn baby out of his car seat carrier, straightened his clothes, and walked down the hallway as the chime of the grandfather clock rang out. Just months prior, I'd gone down that same hallway while terrified to tell Dad about my pregnancy. I was thankful that the current walk was one of great excitement and joy. As I made my way into Dad's room, he had such a look on his face, a good one. I can't adequately explain it, but I know he was happy. God answered another prayer, that Dad would be there to meet his grandson.

Dad's first words were, "Come on doctor. Come here, doctor!" He held his arms out for him. As I laid my baby boy on my daddy's chest, he looked at me and said, "Stay close to me." He didn't want to twitch or have a spasm and hurt him. Dad immediately started kissing the baby and patting him as my brother, my sister, and I watched with grateful hearts. We talked about how quick labor and delivery were and he was glad because I "didn't have to go through all that pain" for long. As we stood there, he said, "This is my daughter, and my son, and my grandson." Looking down at the baby, he added, "Isn't that something?"

Dad scolded me just a little when he said, "This is only the second time I've talked to you since you've been gone." I chuckled to myself before assuring him that I called several times, but he was asleep during most calls, so we had only spoken once while I was in the hospital. As he held the baby, we snapped photos with a disposable camera to capture every precious moment. Looking at my siblings and me, Dad said, "I had the privilege of all three of you being on this big ole' belly." He continued to whisper to the baby about how they would have secret talks.

Not long after this, Mom returned home from her doctor's appointment. As she walked down the hallway to come into the room where all of us were, Dad playfully balled his fist up and shook it a little at Mom to keep her from coming to get the baby. It felt wonderful to have my whole immediate family and our new addition all in the room together. We didn't know how long it would last, but we intended to make the most of each moment the six of us had together on the earth.

Every day, either my brother or I would take the baby into the room with Dad and lay him on Dad's chest. He enjoyed it to the fullest. He wrapped his frail arms around my son's swaddled infant body, closed his eyes, and prayed over him. One time, I caught Dad in his own world holding the baby; he just whispered so softly to him. I couldn't hear everything he said, but he blessed and spoke life over him. Here and there, I'd hear Dad call out, "Mese, he's moving" or "Mese, the baby's stirring." So I'd quickly get him because Dad could hold him while he laid on his chest, but he couldn't lift him or move him much. I'm most grateful that we have some of those moments recorded to watch them over and over again.

Days after my son's birth, Mom called Dad's visiting hospice nurse because Dad began having subtle involuntary arm movements and didn't know the cause of them. When she arrived, the nurse sat Mom and me down at our dining room table. She was a sweet lady and she had visited and taken care of Dad a few times per week for a little while. As Mom and I sat at the table, the nurse handed us both a pamphlet about saying goodbye, loss, and grief. Confused, I stared at the folded paper oddly, I had questions. I needed her to clarify why she gave us that information. I wasn't ready to say goodbye, experience loss, or grieve. I absolutely did not want to sit at that table while she read those words off the paper. *God has the final say.* We would ride it out until the end, no matter what that looked like.

It'd become too hard to get him to his appointments at that point. Sadly, I watched as my brother-in-law or Dad's right-hand elders from our church picked Dad up like a baby and carried his feeble body down the hallway, through the living room, and into the car. It was not only stress on Dad's body but also stress on the strong, abled bodies that carried him. And while the blood transfusions helped, they were not the cure for Dad's illness.

Mom called my sister, who was at work, and told her that Dad wanted to talk to all of us. When she got there, we gathered ourselves in his room. The nurse informed us that the movements were caused by the lack of blood production in his body. She also said that the blood transfusions were prolonging or delaying the inevitable. Her words hit like a ton of bricks. *Delaying the inevitable?* Dad reminded us that he'd been receiving blood transfusions for a while but recently he needed them more frequently. There was the option of him getting another transfusion, so he asked our opinion of what he should do. I said something along the lines of, "Dad, I can't answer that." Ultimately, my sister and I opted for him to have another transfusion. We wanted him with us for as long as possible. After the conversation, my sister and I left the room, but my brother stayed behind. He wanted to talk to Dad privately. During their conversation, he told Dad that we'd been doing a lot of praying and it would be hard on him to go get another transfusion. He felt like at that point, we should turn it over to God. After said conversation, Dad called us back in. He was tired and it was all hard. He fought for over five years and more aggressively for the last two or so. He made his decision and let us know that he thought he would "just go on and give it up." Although this wasn't what we wanted, we understood. There was a point when Dad lifted his hands to God while praying and reiterated his heart's sentiments, "God, my life is in Your hands."

Fifteen

There were no more blood transfusions after March 1st, it was just a matter of time before God healed him. One morning, I sat in my room holding my precious newborn, as two of Dad's friends, the owner and a staff member of the funeral home, walked down the hallway to his room. When they approached his doorway, I heard Dad say, "Hey! Y'all too early." Laughter burst out from everyone, including Dad. Surely, they weren't there to take him. They were there to visit their friend whom they had worked with during funerals at our church and the funeral home over many years. Some people knew his time of transition grew closer, so there were many visitors–none of which warranted such a funny response. Dad's humor was unmatched. I'd experienced it my whole life; I was glad for the smiles and warm, fuzzy laughter, especially then.

Despite finding room to laugh, the reality was that Dad's time was nearing. The evening of Tuesday, March 8th, Dad's spasms were distressing to watch as they'd grown more intense. His left arm shook. The same arm raised in the air, above his head, and continued to shake and move his frail body. Mom was fearful regarding certain things anyway, so this didn't sit well with her at all.

I mean, it didn't sit well with any of us, but it was to the point that she could not sleep in the bed with him that night. What we watched was just what the visiting hospice nurse communicated to us about his heart working extremely hard to pump the little blood he had left throughout his body. The spasms looked painful and terrifying and happened often. We were told that it was normal for one to experience this when close to death.

Mom made a pallet of blankets on my baby boy's nursery floor. It was just a few feet from the room she and Dad shared for the past 35 years. As I walked by the room, I noticed her preparing it and went in to talk with her. She didn't want to wake up next to him to find out he had transitioned during the night. This is how she had to deal with that part. I just didn't want her to sleep on the floor, so I told her to take my bed. She appreciated the offer but refused because she wanted me to sleep well while I could. I'd be up throughout the night with the baby in my room. She also didn't want to get too comfortable or fall into a deep sleep just in case Dad needed her.

That night, the baby woke up only once to nurse. After he was full, I burped him, changed him, and laid him back down. He was sound asleep. Taking advantage of a sleeping baby, I laid down, reached over to my nightstand, turned the light off with one simple touch, and drifted off to sleep.

The sound of Mom's yelling and frantic footsteps beating down the hallway pierced through the silence and the darkness. My eyes popped open up and my heart immediately pounded, shaking my body. *Was he gone?* I braced myself, jumped up out of bed quietly to not disturb the baby, opened my door, and made a sharp turn right just to witness an awful sight. There in my parents' doorway, I stopped in my tracks while watching Dad's body convulse. Partially reclined in his bed as usual, his left arm rattling in the air and above his head, Dad's eyes rolled up in his head and the sound…it was paralyzing. It haunted me for a long time afterward. At a loss for what to do, I involuntarily started praying in the Spirit as the tears streamed down my face. My brother stood at Dad's bedside to comfort him. He'd swab his mouth and lips with wet sponge swabs and carefully give him water through a straw if needed. He prayed within himself, *God, not like this. Don't let him die like this.* There was nothing we could do to help him. I just stood there, watching his body shake uncontrollably and listening to the struggle in his body escape through his mouth.

All of a sudden, I heard Mom in the kitchen crying, so I raced down the hallway to her. I made a sharp right into the kitchen, dimly lit by the bulb above the sink. She sat with a wet face, on the stool, fumbling with the corded landline phone. When someone from the hospice nurse line picked up, all she could say through her distress was, "My husband is so sick. He's so, so sick. Please help him. He's just so sick." My heart bled for her. *My poor mom.* I heard the nurse asking Mom questions, she just couldn't utter the words to answer them. With a heartbreaking sigh, she handed me the phone. I quickly put the phone to my ear to answer the nurse. I told her Dad's name, gave her other necessary information, and described the situation while Mom sobbed. I did my best to stay calm and professional to not delay someone getting there to help. She had me make other calls to some of the elders, family, and church family. Our house would soon be flooded with people.

Dad continued to convulse nonstop. Mom cracked the bedroom windows so he wouldn't get too warm. He heard Mom's sniffles, and I'm sure he felt her worry. He said, "Stay with me Veet. I'm okay," with a weak, trembling voice. She replied that she was there. Amid this uncertain and tragic situation, Dad still looked out for his wife's and family's well-being. He was able to ask for water and talk, but his body would not stop convulsing with his arm raised above his head.

All we could do was keep him comfortable. My sister arrived, and Dad was able to speak to her and have a small conversation. At some point, my baby boy started stirring. So I grabbed him, went into the living room, and nursed him. The doorbell rang frequently, so I covered the baby with a blanket to go answer the door while people came in to see about Dad. Some of the elders, deacons, and friends gathered around his bed and prayed. The nurse got there after a while and an ambulance was called to transport him. He was under palliative care at home, but we could no longer take care of him there due to the convulsions. Instead of going to a hospital, he was to go to hospice for comfort care until God healed him. The ambulance took quite a while to arrive, a couple of hours. Thinking back on it, I wonder if the nurse thought Dad was going to pass and that's why the ambulance took so long. Dad convulsed the entire time. It had been hours since I was awakened in the darkness of the wee hours of the night when the whole ordeal began. God was definitely in the midst and saw him through. Once the ambulance arrived, he was given medication to calm his body and stop the movement. He was then carried out to the living room by the paramedics in a white sheet (the stretcher wouldn't fit past my mom's china cabinet at the end of the hallway) and strapped to the stretcher that sat in the living room. They covered Dad's body and the top of his head with sheets and blankets because it was still cold outside. It was into the morning of Wednesday, March 9th, as dawn approached. I observed with a heavy heart as they wheeled Dad out of our home–the home he built with Mom for the past 35 plus years, unsure if he would return.

Mom rode in the ambulance with Dad. I immediately thought about the health of my newborn because I wanted to go out to the hospice center to be with everyone. I also didn't want to put him at risk or amid germs. I called his pediatrician, explained the situation, and she gave me advice. I was to keep him strapped to me in the body carrier and drape a blanket over his head. I was comfortable with that so I got us ready. I rode with my brother out to the center that I had only been to once before. Even though hospice was known to be the place where patients go for the last days of life for comfort care, I knew it didn't always happen like that. We visited someone who actually came out of hospice and went back home; I was hopeful for Dad, even though the physical signs pointed toward him going to his heavenly home.

The facility was well put together. They were very intentional about it being a place of peace and tranquility. It housed a cozy, neat, and clean library that was semi-private. I remember soothing music playing over the speakers or coming from the piano. It produced a sense of calm and alleviated negative emotions that families may feel while there. The decor provided the patients and visitors with a homey feel.

Once getting into Dad's room, it was very quiet and there were trickling water sounds in the background. I sat next to his bed, looked around, and soaked it all in. It was like we were in another hospital. While we sat there and talked, Dad's speech was sort of slurred. He asked me if I could help him get up to go sit in the chair. Many times before, I had, but this time, it hurt my feelings that I couldn't. I felt so bad because that was one of his last requests of me and I was unable to grant it.

Numerous people came to visit that same day. From his deathbed and with a sound mind, Dad gave clear directions for the church. God knew. As the evening rolled in, he fell into a coma which left him unable to interact with those of us around him. Going home that night felt indescribably empty. Not only was it very late when we got in, the uncertainty of everything and having been at the center all day, was taxing.

For the next two days, Thursday and Friday, we spent most of our time with Dad. Even though he wasn't able to talk to us, we were told he could hear us, so we talked to him, laid the baby on his chest and held him there, and made the best of everything. He had many out-of-town guests, and various people brought us meals, snacks, and drinks as we were consumed with sticking by Dad's and each other's sides. There were nice family areas with TVs, tables, sofas, and chairs too. There was one we sort of claimed as ours, not far from Dad's room. I utilized the quiet and secluded areas of the library to unstrap my son from my body, feed, change, and burp him. While doing so, I prayed. It's funny because looking back, I didn't see this as the end, it was just where we were then.

On that Friday night, many saints, family, and friends gathered all around his room. We sat in chairs in somewhat of a circle in the dimly lit room. We recalled and sang some of Dad's favorite songs. We reflected on some of the precious memories we shared with him. Some spoke about the impact he had on their lives. You could feel the love from one heart to another in that space, but at the same time, you could sense the heaviness. We worshiped together, shed a few tears, and shared in laughter.

When the room cleared out, I took a moment to just be with Dad. I pulled the chair up to the bed, but most of the time, I stood. I stood there as close as I could because I wanted to make sure he heard me. Not long prior, I heard that sometimes loved ones hang on because of the instinctive desire to live and because of their attachment to family. Also, I heard or read that sometimes the person who is near death needs to know that it's okay to go. I didn't know how true all of that was, but I certainly didn't want him in pain or lingering because of us. He had great rest to enjoy; he had suffered enough. Standing there in strength only God could provide, I began to thank him. I thanked him for the lessons he taught me, for the godly life he lived, for the example he provided, and for his love, among other things. When I finished, with a deep breath and a brave heart, I told him it was okay to go. Quietly wiping a few tears from my eyes and stabilizing my voice so he wouldn't hear it tremble, I reminded him that we would miss him tremendously, but I reassured him that we would be okay. He had given us a lot to work with, if you will. He taught us about Jesus through his preaching and teaching, but he showed us Jesus through the sermon of his life. Yes, it would be hard, but we would make it through because he showed us how to live in Jesus too.

Sixteen

The next morning was Saturday, March 12th, and I debated about going up to the hospice center due to the possibility of there being more visitors than usual. I deeply desired to go be with Dad and the rest of my family, but I also wanted to keep the baby away from large crowds, if possible. I was not getting much sleep because of nighttime feedings, bondings, burpings, and changings. It was good for the baby and me to rest.

I was supposed to get my hair rebraided sometime that day as well, but I decided to cancel the appointment. In my mind, I thought that if something happened to Dad, I didn't want to wear braids to his funeral. I preferred to wear my hair down with some curls as he liked, for such an occasion. My brother called while he was at the center to see if I wanted him to pick me up to take me there. I told him that I would call him when I was ready, possibly later in the day. I got off the phone and laid there as the baby slept peacefully. I drifted off into a light sleep, but I'm not sure for how long. During this sleep, God gave me another dream. In the dream, I laid in bed just as I was in real life. I was on my right side, the phone on the nightstand beside the bed, the baby a couple of feet behind me on the other side of the bed, and I slept peacefully.

Suddenly, I heard the house door open and it alerted me. I thought to myself, *I just got off the phone with him, so why would he come to get me now? Dad must've passed.* I looked out my bedroom door toward the hallway and saw my brother walking toward my room with another person walking behind him. I couldn't see the person enough to recognize them, but I knew they were there. Standing in my doorway, he looked at me and said, "He's gone." Then the dream ended.

What felt like moments later, I was jarred out of sleep by the sound of the house door opening and by the dream I'd just seen, playing out before my eyes in the physical realm. Just like in the dream, I thought to myself, *I just got off the phone with him, so why would he come to get me now? Dad must've passed.* I watched in amazement and shock as it all unfolded. Once my brother reached my doorway and said, "He's gone," I was able to recognize the person behind him as she sweetly came into my room to help me get the baby and myself ready to go to the center. It was my dear sister-friend who cared enough to think ahead to help me during the unsettling news. I was calm though because I'd seen it and I guess in a sense, I knew it was coming. We quickly got the baby ready and the diaper bag packed. I got myself together all while the news hadn't fully sunk in. I had things to do, so I could not be emotional and it didn't occur to me to be.

You know, it's astonishing how your body and mind know to press through during times like these. This isn't always the case, but I believe it's a part of coping. I went into business mode because a lot would happen and get set in motion between then and his funeral. I was in disbelief as we rode out to be with the rest of our family. My heart pounded as the fear of life without Daddy became more real.

Once we arrived, I walked to his room for the last time. I spent the previous three days there, but it felt longer. Maybe it was because I hadn't heard his voice in three days or because he had been in a coma that long. It could have felt that way due to the anticipation of the unknown. I walked down the hallway and made a right turn to go down another hallway. Some of Dad's visitors were still there because they were visiting when he transitioned or heard and came to be with us. I passed them on my way, approaching Dad's door at the end of the hallway on the right, next to a locked emergency exit. That walk was worse than the one to his room to tell him I was pregnant. The previous walk involved a dialogue between the two of us.

The current walk was to see my lifeless father laying there in a hospice bed, never to have a dialogue with me again. I walked in the doorway, and the few people who were in there somewhat cleared the room after we spoke to each other, to give me a minute. I walked up to his bedside, the same side I had poured my heart out to him on the evening before, and I stared at his shell—it was surreal. As I looked at him, it was bizarre to me that he wasn't breathing. I knew he wasn't there, but I'd never seen him not breathing. For the last 61 years, my father's lungs were filled with my heavenly Father's breath, now they weren't.

I laid next to him as a little girl and he held me close with his arm. While listening to the beat of his heart, I felt and watched his white t-shirted stomach go up and down with each inhale and exhale. At times, I slowed my breathing to match his. Every now and then, I unintentionally fell asleep while breathing his same rhythm, safe in his security.

Gone were the days of Dad randomly asking me, "What do you think of the price of eggs in China?" No longer would I hear, "You think you'd like to eat when you learn how?" after dropping food while attempting to put it in my mouth. I would never again hear him call me while he stood in front of the bathroom door mirror, to fold down and fix his dress shirt's collar after he tied his tie. I admired how neat and put together he was and after fixing his collar, I checked him for any loose threads or untidiness. I wouldn't find him sitting at the dining room table studying the Word in the middle of the night anymore. I could go into his office and sit in his chair, but I would never again find him there.

We shared a love for ice cream. I mentioned earlier how Dad introduced it to me. Before he could no longer drive, we would go get ice cream quite frequently before Bible study or mid-week service. He enjoyed it and looked forward to going–it seemed to lift his spirits some from the suffering in his body. Down through the years, after some evening services, Dad would announce from the pulpit for the congregation to load up the church bus because he was taking everyone for ice cream. We would go caravan style. Whoever wanted to ride the bus could, plus there were families who drove. When he found a new ice cream place, he would take us. We snapped photos, sat around, laughed, and talked while enjoying our cold treats. A lot of bonding took place. The genuine love Dad had for his flock showed through his actions, ice cream nights were just one of the many ways. And just like that, ice cream with Daddy (Bishop) were precious memories to hold onto, and no more would be created.

Before I left his bedside, I noticed something that brought me great joy. The port in his arm was no longer there, no more pain pump. No more pain. He was relieved of his suffering. He was healed, but it created a wound in me. Dad's healing brought a pain that I had never imagined, but I couldn't fully feel it just yet. I could, however, feel a sense of emptiness. As I walked away from his side, I left his room and continued to walk away from the crowd. I wanted to just breathe and attempt to process the facts. I'd never suffered a loss like this, one of a person this close. The signs were apparent for some time, so we knew death was a great possibility, but no matter how much knowledge you have, you are never prepared for the moment a loved one transitions or for its effect during the days and years afterward.

After returning to his room, I knew when the funeral home staff came that day, it was not for a visit and Dad would not crack a joke. Unfortunately, the funeral staff wasn't "too early" again. I watched them wheel the dark body bag, on a gurney, out the emergency exit next to his room door. They slowly loaded him into the hearse, and I stood there watching the tail lights as they drove off with my Daddy. *Now what?* The whole world kept going on while my family and I could only focus on our loss. It was such a great loss, one that would stick with me for the rest of my life.

The week leading to his funeral would be extremely busy. It started once we arrived home from the hospice center. Much of our church family came to our house, to help us prepare for the visitors and family coming in from out of town. They all pitched in to help us; but after they returned to their homes, we were left to sit with our feelings.

The next day, my grandmother came in from three hours away to stay with us until after the funeral. It meant a lot that she came to be there for my mom. She was able to bond with her newest great-grandson, and she watched him while we went to the funeral home to make Dad's arrangements. It was refreshing to have her with us.

That week, there was a flood of visitors who brought and sent chicken, desserts, fruit baskets, chicken, cards, flowers, more chicken, meals, and so much more throughout the week. People came to sit, reminisce, and keep us company. Writing Dad's obituary was a time of reflecting on his life, his accomplishments, and his heart. We picked out his final undergarments, suit pants, dress shirt, tie, socks, shoes, and robe. The base of the robe was white with black velvet panels, a white cross embroidered on each panel, in the front. The three black, velvet bars on each arm, signified his doctorate status. My brother took great care in shining Dad's black and white dress shoes. Dad was an eloquent dresser–not loud, but sharp. He liked good, quality clothes and wanted them for his family too. We wanted to make sure we honored him, even in his final appearance. All of this led up to his services the following weekend.

Dad's wake was the evening of Friday, March 18th, and his homegoing celebration was the morning of Saturday, March 19th. The morning of the funeral, I put on a beautiful, off-white suit with pretty designs at the top that Dad had bought me. I hadn't worn heels in months, but they were also off-white to match my outfit. I wore my hair down with flowing curls. My son wore black and white baby dress pants, a white dress shirt, and a black velour vest, with a little reddish-maroon clip-on tie. His little feet kept warm with white socks, no need for shoes. After I moisturized and brushed his hair, it was time to leave for Dad's service.

I came down the hallway to the sound of a familiar voice. I turned the corner into the living room to see Jon's (my ex-boyfriend's) mother, and I couldn't believe my eyes. I hadn't spoken with her or Jon for quite some time, but they heard about Dad and wanted to come. My heart fluttered, just a little when I saw Jon. I remembered how close they were, and I knew Dad greatly impacted Jon's life for the better. Dad had that gift; through

God, he changed lives.

Before loading up to leave, everyone gathered in our front yard, which still had deep tire tread marks. We stood there, needing God's strength, so we prayed together. These moments seemed dreamlike–I went through the motions still in disbelief.

When we arrived at the church, the parking lot, the lots across the street, and the streets themselves were filled and lined with cars. There was room for our limo and family cars to park, but we couldn't even go in the main door of the church building because attendees were everywhere, blocking the entrance. The funeral directors had us go into the front entrance and the side door of the sanctuary. It took a while for my very large family to file into the many rows of reserved seats in the front of the church. People were tightly packed into the pews, wooden folding chairs were occupied in the aisles, and there wasn't any more standing room in the back.

As service started, loud praise to God for Dad's life was lifted. I was thankful for his life and grateful that he was no longer suffering, but my body and heart didn't feel like praising Him. I sat there on the first row, hurting while looking at his body, just a few feet away from me. His casket was surrounded by countless floral arrangements, spread through the width of the sanctuary. There was a cute stuffed bear that a child from the neighborhood brought to lay at the altar too. Against my feelings, I clapped my hands and gave God praise, simply because He was (is) worthy.

I sat a little nervously during the first part of the service because I was on the program to give a family tribute. I jotted notes about Dad on the back of the funeral program as songs, remarks, condolences, scripture readings, and music went forth. I witnessed him do the same when he gave a eulogy sometimes. When it was time for me to speak, I walked up the few pulpit stairs, over to the podium, and looked out at the fullness of the crowd. To see how this poor boy from Illinois affected so many people spoke volumes. I recall Dad telling me stories of how when he was a boy he was embarrassed when he was dropped off at home. He had whoever drove him, drop him off a few houses down from where he lived to avoid them seeing his house. The odds were stacked against him before he entered the world, but God had a plan for his life that touched everyone there and plenty who weren't. He boasted in the Lord and said what his mama's razor strap couldn't do, God did! He often spoke about how God brought him from the gambling table to the pulpit, from the gutter most to the uttermost. His life was a beautiful testimony of God's redemptive power at work. You could hear it each time someone spoke of him or just by taking a look around.

As I mentioned, with Dad being bi-racial, there were, most likely, times in his life when he felt like he didn't fit in anywhere. I am sure many people, bi-racial or not, have had similar feelings at some point or another. The same was probably true with his pastoring because it comes with a level of isolation. Satan has a way of making people feel alone from every single person on the face of the earth. He is good at his job. He certainly made me feel quite alone during my pregnancy and afterward. I clung (and still cling) to one of Dad's quotes, "All by myself but never alone."

I anticipated peoples' judgments of me because I had just given birth a few short weeks before–unwed. Some comments and conversations got back to me throughout my pregnancy, but in those moments, I had to forget it all and speak with confidence to honor him. I spoke of childhood memories, vacations, his sense of humor, his wit, his dedication to the Word and the Church, and finally bits and pieces of his sickness. Although I knew Dad could no longer hear my voice, I concluded by thanking Him for standing and told him I'd see him in the morning.

As I walked away from the podium, applause broke out and it felt good to hear. Relief met me upon getting back to my seat, and Mom leaned over to whisper that I did well. I wanted to do Dad justice, and although his life spoke for itself, my words gave a glimpse of our personal life with him. He wasn't a person who lived life in public one way and in private another. What you saw anywhere was the way he lived everywhere.

My sister read Dad's obituary and my brother gave the eulogy. He wore Dad's other black and white robe that was almost identical to the one Dad had on. I prayed for him because this eulogy was not like any other he would ever give. It was entitled, "This is Why I've Been Living Right." He told the audience about the intimate moments we had just a few months prior in Dad's church office, when Dad spoke those same life-changing words to us. I watched in amazement as he allowed God to use him through his grief, for such a time as this. The strength he displayed, was the same strength Dad operated in when he eulogized his mother just five years before. In his conclusion, he told about the dream of comfort God gave me with the angel taking Dad by the hand, out of our circle, and into the heavens.

At the end of the service, what seemed like hundreds of people filed to the front for their last viewing of Dad and to greet the family. There was such an outpouring of love that we hugged countless people as they came by our seats to give condolences and offer prayers. After all the visitors were finished, the time came for our family to tell him goodbye and it was hard, it was really hard. I rubbed Dad's hand as if he could feel it, but I knew it was my own attempt to grasp at comfort. The once warm, life-filled hand was now cold, frail, and lifeless—my heart ached. It came time for Mom to close the casket, so she followed the funeral director's instructions by placing the overlay just at Dad's neck, his face still exposed. She placed her hand on the lid of the casket, gazed upon her husband of the last 35 plus years for the final time, and with God's strength, closed it.

We proceeded to the cemetery directly following the service. Eloquent words were given, scriptures read, and Dad's body committed back to the dust. I sat in the green gravesite chair with my little cousin on my lap as we sang one final song before leaving, and it triggered my emotions. The words to the song "...when we all see Jesus, we will sing and shout the victory," accompanied by the fact that I was leaving my daddy there, was too much for me. It was then that grief hit me and I lost it. I tried my best to contain it by telling myself that it was almost over and to wait to let it all out at home, in private. It seemed as if the more I fought it, the more the tears forced themselves out. I ducked down behind my little cousin's back and did an absolutely ugly cry. I sobbed from my gut as quietly as I could and felt people surrounding me and laying hands on me. They prayed for God's comfort to be upon me and shed tears themselves. It was exactly what I didn't want to do—cause a scene. My best friend/cousin's mom was one of the voices I heard around me. She handed me a very fancy, red handkerchief with lace around the perimeter. It caught the evidence of my grief and I desired so badly to wipe the sadness away. After a while, I gained my strength and we headed back to the church for the repast. The empty feeling prevailed and sank in as we crossed over into a new way of life.

Dad preached a message once about how we should be like a palm tree. Palm trees aren't ordinary in their make-up, they are unique, and their composition is incomparable to other trees. He gave a beautiful illustration of how when storms come, palm trees bend but they don't break. After the storm passes, the tree snaps back into place and then stands strong and tall. When the winds and rain of our lives try to snap us in half, we will bend, but we must not break. My family was in the middle of weathering our worst storm. Our leaves almost touched the sand as our trunks bowed in grief but eventually, just like the palm tree, we would snap back.

Seventeen

In life, there will be several new beginnings, some of which we welcome and others we despise. In general, the loss of a loved one is in the latter category because death is a result of sin–I believe we grieve sin, the original catalyst of death. Because sin entered the world, it is the root cause of the suffering we face today. We suffer as the result of not just death but also sickness, hatred, the illusion of self-control, divorce, rebellion, and the list goes on. At the root of it all, is sin. I am not saying that you or a loved one became ill or died as a punishment for your personal sins. I'm not saying that at all. What I am attempting to convey is that when sin entered the world, it brought consequences (the bigger picture).

In our humanity, we grieve our losses and all they entail. Our minds think about how we are separated from our loved ones, never to see them again on earth. The void that separation leaves can be so deep, leaving us stricken with sadness and sometimes depression.

Jesus took on all of our sins on the cross and grieved because that sin would separate Him from His Father–God. Even though Jesus was without sin, His love for us was so great, that He paid the price for our sinful actions and took the guilt for us. He related to every area of our lives in which we hurt because He experienced and bore it all. Even though this is a fact, what Satan will do is try to make one feel alone during traumatic times or times of transition. He makes it seem like no one can relate to you or makes it seem as though your situation is unique and hasn't ever been experienced.

Another of Satan's tactics is to steer you away from dealing with your feelings or to nudge you towards subtle pacification of dealing with them on a surface level. This can look like busyness, distractions, and talking about all the good memories but not dealing with how the loss is affecting you.

After Dad's funeral, I was consumed with caring for my newborn, being a good mother, and finding a babysitter for when I returned to work not long after. I was ignorant of needing to sort through my feelings, so for the most part, they were suppressed. It never dawned on me to see a therapist to help navigate this part of my life. My world changed drastically, not once but twice in less than a month. Little did I know, this had the potential to catch up with me. I just kept going because there was still life to live. My son was the life that kept us going when death lingered and then claimed my daddy. He was the sweetest reminder of God's grace and love for me during that dark season. God sent him to me–right on time.

At night, the cry of my hungry baby would awaken me, and I would nurse him while hot tears rolled down my face. As I would sing one of Dad's favorite songs to him, the lyrics would comfort me, "Up above my head, I hear music in the air…I really do believe there's a God somewhere." Because of what I had witnessed in Dad's life, I knew God was still God despite my circumstances. One night, I woke up and my heart was so heavy that I made my way to Mom's room–what used to be Mom and Dad's room. I walked the short distance through the dark, Mom laid on her side of the bed, and Dad's side remained empty. Sadness overwhelmed me as grief spilled out onto my cheeks. I sobbed with everything in me and crawled into bed next to her. It must have jarred her because she sat up quickly to comfort me. All I could utter through tears was, "I want my daddy!" Mom missed him too, we all did but believed that with time, it would get easier to do life without him.

At what felt like random times, Dad used to call us together for family prayer. Growing up, I didn't appreciate the disturbance to my TV time or to whatever else I deemed more important than prayer. When I got a little older, I understood the importance of us praying together as a family, not just as individuals. Prayer was key in binding us together as a close-knit family, but because Dad was no longer with us, we hadn't prayed as a family for some time. One evening, my sister was over for a visit and I called a family prayer. I wept at the thought of it being the first one without him, we all felt the void of his presence. One thing we didn't really do was talk about our feelings or process them together to support each other, but we prayed. God kept us.

Life continued to go on as I made my way back to school to honor the promise I made to Dad. I was determined to make him proud even though he wouldn't be there to see me walk the stage at my college graduation. I had about two years before I would finish and keeping up with actually going to campus, school assignments, and work presented themselves more difficult with a child. While sitting at the computer typing some of my papers, I would look down at my baby boy, who slept peacefully, securely cradled in my crossed leg, and I knew I had to keep going. I knew that I could better provide for him with a good teaching job once I graduated. Some days were easier than others, but God provided me with a wonderful babysitter who had known me since before I was born. I never had to worry about my baby being mistreated. On a few occasions, when my babysitter was out of town, I had to take my son to class with me because my mom and siblings were working. I made it through because I had tunnel vision–my mind was set on giving it my all.

When it came time for me to take the required teaching tests at the end of 2006, I involuntarily came to an abrupt halt. I had never been a great standardized test taker, but that test tested every piece of my patience and endurance. It was either pass or fail. The first time I took it, I failed both parts. I was close to passing but was still discouraged because I worked so hard to get there. My world shook just a smidge because I had to now spend a couple more hundred dollars to retake them. I wouldn't be able to start student teaching without passing those tests. I persevered, signed up to retest as soon as I possibly could, and studied more only to pass one part and not the other. Worry started to rise.

In mid-January of 2007, I started taking one class that paired with student teaching and got the ball rolling to teach that winter semester. All of this was done in the hopes that I would pass the second part of the test. I scheduled it in time to have results before my teaching assignment was scheduled to begin. I studied harder, sometimes into the wee hours of the morning, only to find out I failed it a third time. I was crushed, hurt, and confused. I was forced to drop my class and cancel my student teaching assignment. Sitting out that semester made me question my abilities as well as my call to be a teacher. I had already sat out of school for the winter 2005 semester to give birth and during that same semester, I ended up losing Dad. I wanted to finish school, but at that point, I didn't know if I actually would.

God gave me the strength to test for a fourth time a few weeks later and I implemented new studying strategies. I figured that I wasn't doing something right, but I knew the material. I earned great grades my entire life–honor roll before college and dean's list in college. I took it and guess what happened, I failed! For the fourth and what I thought was the final time testing, I failed it and couldn't have been more discouraged. I said things like "I guess it's just not meant to be," and "I put in all this work for nothing. Drowning in hopelessness, I had to forget about the test, college, and everything that came with it. I had to put the promise I made to Dad out of my mind and just breathe because my stress level was too high.

Taking a step back from school, I resumed working at the portrait studio throughout spring; and continued taking care of my son, not knowing if I'd made a five-year-long mistake by attending college. Baffled, I explored walking away from it all. In desperation for direction and clarity, I asked God to help me and show me what to do. In a journal entry dated April 30, 2007, I wrote, "...I was supposed to be student tchg. this semester and graduating on May 12th. Unfortunately, I didn't pass that stupid praxis test again! I'm so stressed about that. Once again, my life in tchg. amongst other things has been put on hold. I was so discouraged and so upset but I have to take it for the 5th time on June 9th. I don't know what else to study! God's gonna have to perform a miracle it seems."

Within a few weeks, I went to a special service we had at my church. After service, God sent a friend to me who asked me how college and testing were going. I explained everything to her. Little did I know, God had already put it on her heart to help me. She told me the plan and for several weeks, she tutored me on test-taking strategies. I knew the material but needed help with confidence to overcome the anxiety of it all, especially since I had taken it so many times. I couldn't express how grateful I was that she was obedient to God and for the time she sacrificed to help me. I no longer wanted to "throw in the towel" because I now had hope that I could conquer the test.

On June 9, 2007, I attempted it a fifth time using the learned strategies. A couple of weeks later, the envelope containing the results was in my hand. I stood in the dining room with my mom, stomach in knots, and at the brink of tears because I was too nervous to open it. I finally opened it, and took a big breath, only to find out that I PASSED by one point! My mom and I celebrated right there! Before I knew it, I shot out of the side door and ran in victory. I ran around the house and the garage several times. "Thank You, Jesus! Hallelujah!" I ran and ran to express my thankfulness and Mom watched with happiness and relief written all over her face. She witnessed my tears and long nights, prayed for me, and supported me through it all. She never left my side or spoke down to me, but rather gave encouraging words and lifted me. Through this trial that lasted over six months, my heavenly Daddy taught me perseverance and reminded me that He hears my prayers and is always with me.

I scheduled my student teaching along with the accompanying class for the fall semester and finally applied for graduation. It'd been a long time coming, but I could finally see the light at the end of the tunnel until I received a disturbing call from the university.

It appeared that I never took two world civilization classes during my freshman year and I would not graduate without them. The victory I celebrated was compounded with feelings of defeat as the news rang in my ears. I told the lady on the phone that I was student teaching that semester and didn't know how I would be able to do it all. The start of the semester was just a week or two away, yet I found myself in limbo again, not knowing if I would be able to move forward. I wondered why I didn't remember to take the classes or how I could be so irresponsible as to not have it all together. I beat myself up because this was not only my future but my son's also. If I had been aware, I would have taken those classes while I sat out the previous semester. I was so crushed after that phone call, I sat in my friend's driveway and cried in my car. Exhaustion did not adequately describe how tired I was of fighting my way through school and through life at that point.

During the past four years, I had been through a great deal of suffering. Some of it was just the result of living in a fallen world and the rest of it was because of my own poor choices. God doesn't just talk to talk–there are specific reasons why He tells us what He does and guides us through His Word. There will be difficulties in following God's design simply because we are human, but when we succumb to Satan's agenda for us, life is that much more difficult. Following Satan's plan, directly or indirectly, will leave you peaceless, hopeless, or with a false sense of hope while going through trials, and will ultimately lead you to destruction. Sometimes we take sin lightly because we don't always see the result of it immediately. But in my dad's eulogy, my brother said, "Living a life of sin is like taking a vacation on a credit card. One day, it will be time to pay up." It's not enough to be "a good person." Even on our best days, our righteous acts are like filthy rags. Through repentance, acceptance of Jesus as our personal Savior, and belief in His death, burial, and resurrection, we receive the gift of salvation. He takes our sins, and we receive His righteousness. We do not have to work for it but rather believe. Salvation is not *works* based; Jesus did the work already. He paid it all! A relationship with Him will produce fruit through the Holy Spirit in your life.

I accepted Jesus many years prior when I was a young teen, but some of the decisions I made (especially during that stretch of four years) didn't reflect my love for Him and they had a ripple effect moving forward. I tried to do things my way instead of operating in and out of who I knew God had called me to be. I fought hard to cut strings with my past, but it's difficult to do so when soul ties are a factor. My life had even been threatened a few times, but it wasn't until God used my toddler's discernment and my protection of him to finally cut the biggest string. On September 9th, I looked in my son's face and made a vow to him that would save my life and ultimately his.

I could see very clearly that for the last several years of my life, I had not been consistently on the right path, but it was hard to stick with my decision to walk away and stay away from a certain relationship. My sister and I sat in her car one evening and she posed a couple of questions to me that would change my outlook. She asked if I thought what I was holding onto was what God had for me. I quickly answered, "No!" She continued (paraphrased), "Do you think by holding on, you're blocking what God has for you?" This question would be one I would apply to many areas of my life for years to come. With the biggest of strings severed, I could move forward but not without the residue of my decisions nor without the yoke they put around my neck. Through this, my heavenly Daddy reminded me that keeping Him as my focus and staying close to Him was key for necessary discernment.

As I sat in my friend's driveway with tears streaming down, what I was faced with was just the icing on the cake compared to what I described above. It was a separate category of my life but affected other areas. With no idea how I would juggle two additional classes,

I searched for options and found that I could student teach during the day and take the classes in the evening. My friend encouraged me to do it and offered much help. That schedule would cause very busy and long days. I would need assistance with the care of my son. It was my only option if I wanted to graduate at the end of the semester. After consulting with my family, I signed up for the additional classes, Japan and China World Civilizations.

Each day, I would get up, get my son and myself ready, and out the door we would go. Sometimes this task was easier than on other days. You never know what could happen with babies and toddlers during that process. A typical day would be to drop him off at the daycare, arrive at the high school by 7:45 a.m., teach, plan new lessons, bond with students, and leave around 4:00 p.m. I felt some mom guilt because after picking him up from daycare, I had to leave him with my mom (most days), brother, or sister, and head to one of the evening classes.

I shed tears and some nights I wouldn't sleep because of preparing detailed lesson plans. I also stayed up because papers needed to be graded or written. I assigned projects to my students and had to complete my college class projects from my professors. As I refreshed myself and read my students' literature, I simultaneously read literature about Japan. It was "bananas." I even developed a scalp condition that was triggered by stress. What seemed to be a never-ending cycle was only temporary, I repeated that to myself and longed for the day that I would suit up in my cap and gown.

On December 15, 2007, around three years after promising Dad I would finish college, I fulfilled it. I walked the stage of my university, medaled by the National Society of Collegiate Scholars, and graduated Cum Laude. All of the late nights, test retakes, sweat, and tears had finally paid off. The process, though I can't comprehend how I got through it successfully, developed me, and prepared me for my next chapter of life. In this, my heavenly Daddy taught me endurance.

Eighteen

Throughout the next several years, I found myself always adjusting to new things and changes that took place. So much happened without me grieving the loss of Dad or without me dealing with chronic and complex traumatic events in my life. After graduating college, I hoped to begin teaching in some capacity, so I quit my job at the portrait studio and began to substitute teach toward the beginning of 2008. I knew I wanted my own classroom, but it was the middle of the school year so not many opportunities were available at that time. In the meantime, I updated my resume and applied for teaching positions for the fall. One day, I called to check on my application and the lady I spoke with said that it may take quite a while for me to get a job in my field. This was a bit of a gut punch because you knew the challenges I faced while pursuing my degree, only to find out that there were no job opportunities available for me. I had a son to care for and bills to pay; so, I prayed about what to do. In the summer, I wouldn't be able to work as a substitute teacher.

Around this same time, a certain someone who I had met in high school in 1999 started showing up more in my life. We were really good friends and hung out as such, off and on, for six or seven years. There was always an interest between us but neither of us acted on it in order to preserve our friendship. In addition, at various times in our friendship, one or both of us were in a relationship with other people. It felt really good to have great conversations and ask each other's opinions or advice without the pressure of performance.

Our friendship started to blossom into something more and both of us felt it. When the time presented itself, our conversations shifted to what we wanted, to the possibility of our lives together, and what that could look like for all three of us. The conversations grew longer and we became closer, but I felt like I needed confirmation from God to move forward. I could see the fruit of his life; there was evidence of him walking with God. Because of the way I saw this heading and progressing, I wanted to make sure I wasn't blinded by love. I asked my mom and brother (and a couple of other trusted individuals) to be my eyes and let me know (at any point) if there was something, anything that they saw that I should be concerned about in my relationship.

You see, the problem with (a part of) my past was that I kept things hidden because I knew I wouldn't get the approval from those around me who loved me to continue in a toxic relationship. I wanted to be in it anyway, so I kept it separate and ended up getting burned. The wound from doing things my way was still open, and healing all the way had not yet happened. I needed just a little bit of help to make sure I was on the right path. I wanted to go about my current relationship the right way, so I was vocal about wanting the approval of my mom and I welcomed her opinion. Most importantly, I prayed to God for guidance.

One night, I asked God to show me a specific thing. Not many times had He answered me so quickly. Moments later, my phone rang and He showed me the very thing I had just prayed for through a conversation. So our relationship continued to progress toward engagement in the summer. I couldn't believe how everything was unfolding before me. I didn't have to guess his feelings for me or his intentions for our lives, nor did I have to force anything with him. He didn't play with my emotions or make me feel bad about my past. My heart felt safe, it had a home in him.

We were happily married the following spring, but there was much to learn about this new chapter of my life but not just mine, all three of our lives. You think you know someone before you marry them and live together, and that's true to a very small extent. This is where most of my married readers will probably laugh because it is the absolute truth. You may enter into marriage with expectations of what it will be like waking up to the person you're so in love with every morning and the bliss you will feel while lying next to them at night. Quite honestly, most enter marriage very naively. I can't speak for everyone, but those who I've heard speak about marriage, have similar stories. One doesn't know what marriage will be like because they have never been married before. Or if one has been married before, the outcome is unknown because the new relationship is with a different person. Either way, we loved each other through it all and knew that with God's help, we would adjust in time.

Let's pivot. So, I'm about to give you a lot of information in the next few paragraphs. I want you to stay with me on this journey without having to read thousands of pages filled with details. Are you ready? Okay, let's go.

In the first few months of adjusting, I was called out of the blue to interview for a teaching position and was hired on the spot. Two short weeks after I started teaching part-time, we welcomed our second beautiful child into the world, as adjusting continued. While on maternity leave, I was super emotional because the baby came two and a half weeks early and I felt ill-prepared. We had health insurance issues through my husband's job, and I had mommy guilt because my attention was split between my oldest and newborn. I received a call from the Board of Education with an offer to teach full-time once my leave was over. I remember silently crying on the telephone because even though I had prayed for a good position, it was at the school I prayed not to go to. Against my feelings and with my husband's counsel, I accepted the position. After only spending six weeks at home with my newborn, which wasn't nearly enough time, I entered the world of teaching at a middle school.

During my first couple of weeks, I experienced way too many emotions. I was excited, happy, grateful, nervous, terrified, and sad, among other emotions. I knew the transition would be a little difficult for my family and me. I also kept in mind how it was a transition for my students too because the school year had already begun, and they had substitutes until I came in early November. I previously shadowed and even subbed in middle school classrooms, so I knew it could be a challenge. Most days after work, I was exhausted but still had to have energy for my family. I cried a lot, mostly silently and in the privacy of my bathroom. But sometimes, while cooking or attempting to do other household chores, I quickly wiped a tear that found its way out despite my efforts to hide it. I felt like no one understood what I was going through except my mom. She offered much encouragement and poured wisdom into me at just the right times.

One day, while the students were switching classes, I felt this wave of missing my baby and a wave of overwhelmedness. I was on hall duty just outside my classroom door and again, I told myself that I better not let one tear out. I felt it coming on and before I knew it, I started crying right in the middle of the hallway. I didn't let one tear out, I let what felt like hundreds out along with the sounds, you know, the ugly sounds that accompany the ugly face. I was deeply embarrassed, so I covered my face with my hands. Suddenly, I felt hands laying on me and heard the familiar voices of two neighboring teachers praying for me, in Jesus' name. As they prayed in the middle of the hallway, I felt God's comforting presence give me peace. God sent those two special women to be there for me in the exact way I needed. They set their jobs aside to intercede for me when I couldn't open my mouth to pray for myself. The relationships I had with them after that day were something special because they weren't just my co-workers, they were my sisters in Christ. Even though I had a rough time at first, I'm grateful that my heavenly Daddy placed me at that school because it was there that He allowed my path and that of one of my very best friend's to cross, the following school year. He gave me a dream about her before we ever had a conversation and it was the beginning of our bond.

As months went by, I became better accustomed to my new life as a wife, second-time mom, and teacher. As more time went by, I gave birth to my two youngest children. Looking back, I was pregnant at some point in each year of our marriage for the first four years. With each blessing came more adjusting–physically, mentally, and psychologically. Two years after the birth of my last baby and when I thought I'd gotten used to life, we made a huge move to another state. My husband, children, and I left everything we knew–our support system, family, jobs, and friends–to pursue a life more than eight hours away. I fought the idea of moving for quite a while until I couldn't fight any longer. The uncertainty of an unfamiliar place kept me from seeing the possibilities that would come from relocation. I was comfortable with my family and friends. I had great people, some of whom I had known most, if not all, of my life. In my search for peace, God showed me that I would have a support system in the place I was going but it would be different from what I was used to. He then confirmed that word through a dear mentor not long after and I felt a little better. He was calling me out of my comfort zone and into the deep. To be obedient to His call, I had to trust Him.

When we settled into our new place, I became sad and homesick. I had never met new people from scratch like that in my life. Someone I knew was always around. In my sadness, however, I was excited to explore the area to see what was out there. The children and I drove around quite a bit and found some cool places to visit. The city was a lot bigger than the one we had moved from.

There was so much to do from registering my children for their new schools to finding great pediatricians and doctors for everyone, to finding a new church home. I was born into the church I grew up in and attended there until we moved, so finding a church home was interesting, to say the least. One huge adjustment that took me longer to come around to was going from being a full-time teacher to being a stay-at-home mom. This was one of the things my husband and I agreed upon before we moved: I would stay home with our youngest two children while my husband worked his new job.

Working offered a small break and time away from my children even if I was teaching other peoples' children. They also went to a great daycare/summer camp program that afforded me much-needed quiet time. I could always turn to my mom for a break by going to her house because she understood me and the pressures of motherhood. Just going to her house was a breath of fresh air because she would often say, "Why don't you go lay down for a while? I've got the kids." I'd go snuggle in her bed, usually on Dad's side, while the incomparable warmth (not the temperature), the familiarity, and the smell of their bedroom brought me great comfort. I would glance at Dad's photo on the wall, pull the covers up over my ear and down my jawline, and miss him before falling into a priceless sleep. After my slumber, the children would have eaten something good and probably made a mess in their playroom. Mom was the absolute best, not just because of everything she did, but because of everything she was. Unfortunately, I was so far away from her that I had to settle for telephone conversations.

That fall, I began having dreams that disturbed me greatly. In the dreams, my dad came back to life, we enjoyed him for a while, but he died again each time. His death would leave me deeply grief-stricken to the point where my sobs translated to the physical realm. I woke up to a soaked pillow while gasping for air and crying out. It had been years since I had that type of grief cry, and I couldn't help but wonder why it came out of nowhere. Little did I know, I would soon find out.

Just five months after our move, there was one phone conversation Mom and I had that changed the course of my life. There were signs of something wrong in her body for a few weeks (possibly more); she had told me about them. You already know what I did! I did a thing most of us do, I googled her symptoms and what I learned confirmed my thoughts. I never told her about my findings, I just prayed for her fervently. I cried out to the Lord, wiped many tears, and pleaded the blood of Jesus over her. I paced my room in prayer, walking back and forth, to and fro, while wrestling with what could have been. Then the day came when Mom was supposed to go to the doctor to see what was going on, and my phone rang that afternoon. She told me that the doctors were about to biopsy the lump they had just found during her mammogram. It was hard for me to grasp the words she spoke. My heart instantly raced and my blood pressure rose as my mind searched for hope. I failed to find it, my head would not wrap around what she said let alone place my hope where I knew it needed to be. I thought back to Dad and how we lost him and couldn't fathom losing Mom at all, especially not to cancer. I already witnessed what it did to one of my parents and my heart ached at the thought of Mom suffering through a similar battle. The date was December 16, 2015, 16 years and three days after I first learned cancer invaded our family the first time. I knew it was back! Ready or not, here we go...again.

Nineteen

During the phone conversation, Mom remained calm which, in turn, made me keep my words and reaction calm. Inside my head was a different story because Satan whispered not-so-sweet nothings in my ear about how my mom would die of the same thing dad died of. I attempted to combat the thoughts by praying to God within myself. My efforts seemed to be in vain due to the sheer panic running through my body, but I fought to elevate my mind above the situation.

Mom expressed how nice the nurses and doctors were to her and she gave me details of her office visit before. My heart ached because I couldn't get to her. I was far away and she had always been there for me, but I could not be there for her in what was probably one of the scariest moments of her life. She may have been scared, but it was not evident in her voice. However, I could tell she was nervous, so I listened to her while my heart was pounding and a headache was brewing at the base of my head. When it came time for her to go back for the biopsy, we got off the phone and I wasn't sure what to do. Helpless, I didn't want to do anything but sit there. There was no time to feel that way, my husband and children depended on me for so much. I felt like my energy was zapped and didn't know if I could function well in the kitchen, so I picked up some sub sandwiches for dinner. Even the small task of ordering food was more challenging than normal because my mind was not there and obviously wasn't thinking completely clearly.

After getting back home, I made sure everyone was settled with their food before taking my sandwich and retreating to our bedroom. Quiet time was much needed. I told my husband what was going on. He gave me the space I needed and kept the children occupied so I could try to process everything. I looked at my sandwich and made myself take bites of it when my husband opened the door to our room and said, "If I were you, I would just try to stay positive about it." That comment sort of struck a chord with me because that's not what I wanted to hear. It didn't make me feel any better. Another problem was that I couldn't even figure out how to do that in those moments. I was super vulnerable and emotional, so the tears streamed down my face, soaking my sandwich. I was unaware of what I needed or how to express anything other than wanting it all to go away and for everything to be better, but all I could do was wait for the test results.

During the wait, my brother, sister, and mom drove the long distance to visit us for a few days before Christmas. I had never gone months without seeing my family, so it made my heart glad to be around them, lay eyes on my mother, and talk to her in person. I could see the change in her physical abilities and her energy levels as she couldn't sleep lying down, nor could she shop as in the past. Nevertheless, we created new memories that I would hold onto for years to come.

In January 2016, the biopsy results showed that Mom was faced with stage four, triple-negative breast cancer which couldn't be operated on, nor could she receive other types of hormone treatments. She opted to have chemotherapy and radiation, but the disease was aggressive. She worked as a teaching assistant for students with disabilities until the time she could no longer work. Treatment had to start almost immediately. I knew that I had to put my eyes on her in person and I desired to help her, but our physical distance hindered me from what was in my heart.

A few weeks later, I asked my sister to send a picture of Mom and she obliged. A few times, I spoke with her during video calls, but we mostly spoke via regular telephone calls. She was tired after her treatments, so I didn't want to call her too much. As I sat and thought of her, I couldn't help thinking of what Dad went through. I hoped she wasn't suffering as he did. Watching him suffer broke my heart, and to know Mom could be in the same situation, crushed it. When I saw the photos of her, my heart dropped.

After I made my desires known to my husband, I was able to fly to see her at the very end of February. In my mind, I wanted to be her hands and feet for the time I was there. I wished to serve and honor her in every possible way, so I thought about the everyday things that she may have had trouble doing because of her condition. I asked God to help me in this endeavor. My brother helped her tremendously, but he was dealing with a chronic condition and vision impairment himself. He also wasn't a woman, and I knew that there were things he couldn't do for her as I could. I was a nurturer like Mom.

Upon landing, I was glad to see my siblings when they picked me up from the airport. It felt good to talk, laugh, and just be in their presence on our way home–the home I was born and grew up in. However, I was a little nervous because I knew Mom's illness had taken more of a toll since I saw her last, and I wanted so badly to not react once there. When we arrived, the three of us walked up the porch steps and after opening the door, my brother told me to brace myself. *Gulp.* As I told you before, I'd seen a couple of photos and even video chatted with Mom, but I guessed that her physical condition was worse in person. When we entered, I was determined to be courageous, so I walked down the hallway to Mom's room with my brave face on. I reached her room and while I smiled outwardly, it hurt to see the effects of cancer in her body, in person.

Mom's head was bowed down and slightly tilted to the left–she couldn't lift it. Her left hand and arm were swollen so much, they were hard to the touch–she couldn't use them. The left side of her face was swollen and puffy, matching the rest of the left side of her upper body. I hugged her ever so gently to not disturb her already uncomfortable state. She smiled, glad to see me and I made sure my facial expression didn't show the internal war I had with my emotions. We talked for quite a while that evening and I told her to use me in those few days I had with her. She could still walk pretty well, but there were some things God laid on my heart to do for her, two of which were bathing her and washing/styling her hair in a way she wouldn't have to deal with it at all.

The next morning, as Mom and I sat in the living room, she gave me very specific errands to run on her behalf. As I wrote, she expressed to me how kind and generous everyone around her had been, she couldn't get over it. I watched her my whole life as she provided daily rides to various neighbors and co-workers, cooked meals to share with others, washed bags of laundry, delivered them to those in need, and the list goes on and on. I told her she was simply reaping what she had sown for so many years. She replied that she hadn't even thought about it like that, the words of a true giver. I created the list which included going to the high school at which she worked to gather her personal belongings and return washed casserole dishes, to caring co-workers, that once contained delicious food.

I drove her minivan to the school, the same school at which I had completed my student teaching over eight years prior. I returned the dishes to each owner and thanked them again. Everyone spoke so highly of Mom and said how much they missed her presence. They also mentioned that they were looking forward to her return, but in my heart, I didn't think she would return. I went to her classroom and packed everything she asked me to pack, before sadly walking out of the building to the car.

I intentionally tried to make the best of every moment with her. I asked God to use me, to help me extraordinarily serve her, and to give me supernatural power to do so because I knew I couldn't do it in my strength. I longed to make sure Mom felt completely overwhelmed with love and God's tender care toward her. To do so, required me to push beyond my feelings along with uncertainties of what was to come and depend on Him in my weakness.

One of those days, I took Mom to the doctor because she was to have a scan. My brother waited in the waiting room while I wheeled Mom to the back. The scan required her to lie still, flat on her back, which she hadn't been able to do in months. I detected some anxiety in her when she heard this. She asked the nurse if I could stay with her during the scan but was told no due to its nature. I explained Mom's hesitation and complication to the nurse, she was very kind and gave us a moment. I walked Mom through a breathing exercise I learned from my doula before my first non-medicated birth. We took a moment to breathe in deeply while saying Jehovah in our minds, followed by slowly and steadily saying Shalom during the exhale. I reminded her that God was with her and it would be over soon. She completed the scan and told me, "It worked."

On a different day, Mom had a radiation treatment. That was the first time I was able to speak with one of her doctors face to face, so I secretly had a list of questions compiled. Before she was taken back for treatment, she told me not to ask a whole lot of questions. She knew me well. After her treatment, they brought her back into the room, and we waited for her doctor. I wrote a little note letting her doctor know that I wanted to speak with her privately after the meeting. Somehow, I slipped out of the room afterward and she met me down the hallway. I told her I lived out of state and Mom didn't say a whole lot to any of us regarding the details of her progress, so I wanted to know where we stood. As she looked at the questions, she graciously answered them and took time with me. From our conversation, I understood that when they diagnosed her the previous month, the cancer was pretty far gone and the chemotherapy she underwent since then, did nothing to slow its progress. The radiation she received was to try to slow it as well as help her be more comfortable, but ultimately there was nothing else they could do. I asked about her prognosis so I could wrap my spinning head around the facts and create a timeline of how long she had left. The doctor said something like every case and every patient is different but from what she could tell, Mom had less than six months. Two months prior, we had just found out something was wrong in her body, just recently found out what it was; and just like that, it was coming to an end. We had a lot to process. As we wrapped up the conversation, Mom was wheeled out of the room towards me, it was time to go home.

She had some fluid in her lungs which made breathing a little more laborious. I remembered when Dad battled cancer, sometimes it was difficult for him to catch his breath in various circumstances. I knew washing Mom's hair would present a challenge because she couldn't lift her head or lean back to let the water run away from her face. Water running into her face would frighten her because she would feel like she couldn't breathe. With all of this in mind, I placed the bathchair in the tub, got her in there, and did for Mom what she had done for me when I couldn't help myself. I took my time, talked her through, and God gave me a strategy for each stage of the process.

When we were finished, it was time to blow dry and style her hair. She was exhausted by this time, so she dozed off in the chair while I proceeded to braid her hair up into a simple bun. It was so unlike her to not have a conversation with me while I styled her hair, another sign of her life slowly slipping away. I'd done her hair for years, usually on some Sunday mornings when she'd wake me up and ask, "Mese, can you get up and throw a few curls in my hair?" Annoyed (and teenagery) because I wanted to continue my slumber, I'd get up to an already hot curling iron and the smell of an open jar of curling wax waiting for me. I created beautiful spiral curls in her hair with a French roll or by themselves, just before leaving for church. I didn't work real fast because I liked to be precise with hair, so sometimes she'd tell me that it didn't have to be perfect. But that day, I braided quickly so she could rest.

I finished her hair, showed her, and she just smiled. She liked it so much and it made her so happy that she got up and walked into the room where my brother was to show him. My heart was so glad to see her light up like that. Even in her sickness and through the suffering endured in her body, she remained completely sweet, gentle, and kind. She told me that sometimes people aren't so nice when they are not feeling good. She expressed not wanting to be that way and God granted her the strength to have the same temperament as always. It was the light I saw in her smile that made me feel like I had honored her during my stay and served her well.

Early the next morning, it was time for me to return home, and it couldn't have been tougher to do so. We snapped pictures and said our goodbyes before my siblings dropped me off at the airport. I had planned to return with my husband and children about three weeks later for spring break. However, until I got back to Mom, I would think about her, call her, pray for her, and wonder about her future.

Twenty

At the end of March, it was almost time to go back home to see and care for Mom, spend time with family, celebrate the Resurrection, and host my sister's baby shower. I ran to a store to grab a few things as we were scheduled to leave a few days later. While choosing a card for my sister, I happened upon baby shower cards from a mom to a daughter. There was one in particular that caught my eye–it was gray and yellow (matching the shower colors), had glitter on it, and the message was beautifully penned. I called Mom to see if she wanted me to get it for her as I knew she couldn't go to a store. My brother answered the phone, but my excitement plummeted as he explained to me that Mom had fallen. He explained what happened and every fiber in me wanted to drop everything and go to her, but I couldn't. I couldn't do anything but listen to my brother with tied hands. He could not lift her and she couldn't use the left side of her body, so it was a bit of a mess. He needed to attend to her, so he got off the phone, and I began to pray that it would work out and that Mom's pain was minimal. My mom had helped me up countless times during my entire life–physically, emotionally, spiritually, and mentally. All I wanted to do was help her and make her comfortable, but I was over eight hours away.

The day finally arrived when we were scheduled to go back home–a long trip. All packed, snacks in hand, we loaded the car, and off we went. I wondered how my children would react to their MiMi's condition. They had seen her three months prior, but a lot had changed that would be difficult to explain to a child without scaring them. It scared me to see her rapid decline, so I knew they would have reservations and worries. My children were used to their MiMi getting on the floor to play games or do puzzles with them. They looked forward to her taking them outside at the sound of the ice cream truck or simply playing in their toy room at her house. Unbeknownst to them, this trip would be different. Although they could still play in their toy room, MiMi wouldn't be able to play with them like before, sit them on her lap, nor could she lift her head.

Once we arrived at Mom's house, I went straight to her room while my younger children followed behind me. You could see a little fear in their faces and actions once they saw her, so Mom told me not to force them to approach her. She said that she used to feel scared around sick people when she was a little girl, so she understood. I felt bad, but they warmed up and gently hugged her and talked with her. There were quite a few questions that came from a couple of them about her condition, so without giving potentially frightening details, I answered them as best I could.

During that trip, Mom needed more help walking as her legs were weakened. A professional caregiver came to assist Mom with bathing and to do a few other things that she could no longer do for herself. On her first day, the nice caregiver came out of the bathroom and softly yelled out, "Is there a Mese? She's calling for Mese." I got up to quickly go to her, thinking something may have gone wrong, to learn that Mom wanted me to bathe her and wash her hair as I had done before.

As a child, when something went wrong, or even if it didn't but I just wanted her, I called for Mom. Her presence seemed to solve my problems, heal my hurts, and bring joy to my day. I shared my good news with her and she was there for me in the not-so-good times. As a child, I also called out for Dad.

There was one specific day when I was between seven and nine years old, I went to a sleepover at one of my best friend's houses. Her room was in the finished attic of their home and it had wooden floors. The morning/afternoon after the sleepover, I walked across the floor to her bed and felt a sharp pain in my foot that stopped me in my tracks. The pain seemed to shoot up through my leg and jolt the rest of my body. I limped the rest of the way to her bed, and looked down at my foot, covered in my purple sock, but I didn't see anything visibly wrong with my sock. I thought I had just stepped on something. Attempting to play a little more, the pain wouldn't subside but seemed to become more intense, so I quickly and carefully took my sock off to see the horrific sight of a short, thick piece of wood sticking out of the ball of my foot. I was shocked and in pain, so my friend helped me hop across the floor and down the stairs to the living room where her mother sat. She took me to who she relied on in times of trouble, but I wanted my daddy. He was who I relied on, and I knew he could help me. A sense of panic masked by a false sense of calm was written on my friend's mother's face. On the couch with my leg and afflicted foot across her lap, I pleaded with her not to touch my foot or pull the wood out. I exclaimed that I wanted my daddy and that he would get it out. In distress, I asked her to just take me home to my daddy, but she thought she knew best. Against my will, she took her fingers, grabbed the wood, and yanked it out of my foot. I winced, but more than anything, I was upset because she pulled it out. My foot bled and I made up my mind that my stay had come to an end. I was not staying there any longer after such a traumatic experience. After the bleeding slowed down, her mother tried to clean up my wound and put a bandage over it to transport me home. I just wanted my parents and was relieved once I arrived home. However, I could tell something still wasn't right with my foot. There is more to this story that I'll share at the end of this book; but just know that for me, my parents made tough times bearable and better.

That's what Mom was experiencing; it was like our roles were slightly reversed because even though there was someone there to help her, she called out for me. As she had done so many times in my life, I went to her (sort of puzzled at the time because someone was already there) to be whatever it was she needed at that moment. The whole ordeal, especially washing her hair, was more of a struggle than it was three weeks prior, but God helped us get through it. I was able to blow-dry and braid her hair again so she wouldn't have to worry about it, but the process of it all wore her out. Most things tired her out extremely easily, just walking could be a taxing task. I noticed how she fell asleep more frequently than before, and she was quieter and more withdrawn when company came to see her.

A family friend came over to visit Mom one of those days. We were all in the living room and he apologized to her for not getting over there sooner to see about her. Mom's response sticks out in my mind about that conversation. She simply looked up and raised her hand and said, "I find no fault." She said more, but the point was that it was okay. She wasn't holding anything against him or anyone else. This statement has stuck with me since then and I have adopted it and applied it to my life. Forgiveness was how she kept her heart pure. I believe her pure heart was the conduit of her seemingly never-changing sweet demeanor through all the challenges she faced from childhood to the present time. "I find no fault," was both refreshing and convicting. It made me admire her all the more but also challenged me to forgive more freely and quickly.

When the wee hours of the morning of Sunday, April 3rd rolled around, it was time for us to travel back to our residence. Before we pulled off, we stopped by Mom's house to tell her and my brother goodbye. I remember sitting in the car, it was just the children and me because my husband had to fly back home for work earlier in the week. The darkness of the night, except for a couple of dimly lit street lights, surrounded me. The thought that the pending goodbyes could be our last, burdened me. That week, I could see her gradually slipping away, but I hung on to the fact that God was a healer and could turn it all around in a moment. Grateful for the time we had spent together and for the conversations that would stay embedded in my memory bank, I dreaded it to end. At the same time, Mom's pain and discomfort weren't what I wanted either. As I made my way into the house, my brother asked me not to wake Mom because that would cause a seemingly longer night for the both of them after we left. The nighttime had recently caused her to become a little frightened, so throughout, she called out to my brother for various reasons. Many times, she took comfort in calling the weather line as it gave her something to do. I had mixed emotions about not waking her because I wanted to tell her goodbye, but I also understood my brother's plight. I agreed not to wake her and made my way back to her bedroom while he watched the car of sleeping children for me. Once I got to her room, I looked on as she slept in her recliner chair, snuggled between her bed and the wall, the warm glow of the lamp on her nearby nightstand filled the corner. She slept with her head bowed and tilted. I quietly went to her, sat on the bed and just stared at her while praying within myself. I snapped a quick selfie with her as I wanted to remember those moments just in case they were our last. I heard my brother, who had come down the hallway, tell me to go ahead and wake her. We never discussed it, but I felt like he understood the turmoil I faced. I hesitated to call out to her because she looked as peaceful as possible while she slept. However, I overturned my hesitation and gently woke her. I let her know that I was sorry to disturb her but didn't want to leave town without saying goodbye. We spoke briefly, I kissed her, and I walked away sort of overcome with a hint of grief. Once I got back to the car, my oldest went inside for goodbyes as well. My mother told him she would do her best to get better.

After departing, I picked up one of my husband's (and my) dearest friends because he so graciously offered to drive us back home. Since my sister's baby shower was the day before and we had lots of family from out of town visiting, I hadn't slept at all. Previously, I had made the trip alone with the children before, but my heart was so grateful for the sacrifice our friend made to ensure we got home safely. My mind was so boggled that as he drove, I drifted off into a deep sleep. At times, consciousness would resurface and I remembered the nightmare occurring in our lives. We stopped once for gas just a couple of hours from our residence, the children didn't budge but were heavily in their slumbers. I knew it was God because the whole ride was smooth, quiet, and filled with much-needed rest.

That afternoon, as soon as we walked in the door, I received a phone call from my siblings. Under the advice of her visiting nurse,

Mom had to be taken to the hospital. My heart did that sinking thing again. She had never been in the hospital while I was alive. She needed to go because the build-up of fluid in her legs began to leak. Our dear friend offered to drive me back to my mom if I needed him to as if he hadn't just driven us all that way. Knowing that we had support like that made a world of difference because it felt like such an isolating time. I decided against going straight back up the highway for various reasons–my children had to return to school the next day, my siblings were with her and would keep me abreast of everything going on, and most importantly, prayer knows no distance. As concerned as I was and as much as I wanted to be by her side, I knew if things didn't turn around, I would need to go back later.

The next morning, I sat on speakerphone listening to what I didn't want to hear during a conference with my siblings and her team of doctors there in the hospital room with Mom. After evaluation and examination, they said there was nothing else that could be done, so palliative care was decided upon. As you know, this wasn't my family's first rodeo with palliative care, so it hit a little harder this go 'round. Mom said (paraphrased), "Let's not get worked up about it, stay calm and trust God." Her oncologist even offered a compliment to my family about how well they were taking the news of everything. Mom being Mom, told my siblings that it was okay for them to put her in a nursing home. She was being what she always was, nice and sweet, even in the midst of all that. She didn't want to be what she considered a burden to take care of at home, but my siblings quickly said "no." Even though I was far away, I thought, "No" because I wanted her to be well taken care of and comfortable. So, arrangements were made to have a hospital bed, an electric lift recliner chair, and a wheelchair delivered to the house and set up in my old bedroom before she came back home. A visiting nurse, a massage therapist, and other caregivers frequented her to ensure her quality of life while on hospice. It was only a matter of time before one of two things happened–God would heal her or God would heal her.

I lived life without Dad for 11 years but always had Mom, so life without both of them was unimaginable. Much of the time that I waited for status updates, I did a lot of thinking and praying. I found myself staring into space more than usual trying to process it all, but life continued as usual around me. One day, my younger children were upstairs playing together, my oldest was on the sofa watching TV, and my husband was sleeping in the next room. I sat at my dining room table, filled with thoughts of her no longer being there. As much as I tried to change my focus, I quickly became overwhelmed and began to sob. I sobbed so heavily that it alarmed my son and he came running to me while yelling, "Mom!" This alerted my husband out of his rest because I heard our bedroom door fly open as he hastily came to me. Sadly, neither of them could rescue me from what I felt in those moments. Although I could barely talk, to reassure them that Mom was still with us, through my gasps for breath, I uttered, "She didn't die." I felt like I caused this uproar in which the heartbeats of those around me kept up with mine, but I couldn't stop the sobs. My husband led me to our bedroom, laid me down, covered me up, and told me to rest. In consolation, he assured me that everything would be okay. I wasn't sure how because life had presented one of the worst-case scenarios at my front door.

On April 19, 2016, I received a phone call from one of my siblings through which the visiting nurse informed me that Mom had hours to days left and that I should come. Instinctively, I went into business mode because there was much to be done before I caught a flight back home. There was no time to be emotional. Throughout the prior two weeks, I prayed and asked my heavenly Daddy to allow me to be with Mom when she transitioned; it was in my heart to be there. After conversing with my husband, I looked for flights that could get me there that evening. To my surprise and by God's hand, I found a non-stop, one-way ticket for only $30. I felt like He was answering my prayers because things were falling in line so that I could get home. That afternoon, I tidied up my home, did some laundry, packed my bags, picked up my children from school, braided my daughter's hair, and confirmed that everything was set for them. I wasn't sure when I would return or if I would return with sad news.

On my flight that evening, I wasn't grateful for the circumstance, but I was grateful that God allowed me to be with Mom as I had asked Him. My sister and my best friend were at the airport to pick me up and it felt good to be with them. Somewhere along the way to Mom's house, I could feel a shift from more of a relaxed state to a nervous one. We stopped by a local store where I grabbed junk food. At the time, I didn't realize I was purchasing and eating because of stress, I thought I just wanted some snacks to have for the night.

Once we arrived, I took my bag inside and got as settled as possible. Without wasting time, I quietly walked into my old bedroom where Mom slept in the hospital bed. Again, her appearance changed some from when I last saw her just over two weeks ago. I put a chair beside the bed and stared at her for a while. Grateful to be there with her, I wanted her to know I was there, but I figured the best thing to do was enjoy the moment of seeing her sleeping peacefully and be there in the morning to greet her when she awakened.

There was a recliner chair at the foot of the bed. I made this my home for the night while the vigil nurse sat in the lift recliner. She and I had a good conversation while I nervously ate my snacks. She answered my questions, assured me of a few things, and at one point she told me I didn't have to stay up but I could go rest. I didn't know what Mom's sleep patterns were like, so if she were to wake in the night, I wanted to talk with her. As a child or even as an adult when I would wake at night, for whatever reason, I could always count on Mom to talk with me whether in person or over the telephone. She was there to comfort me when I was sick and even though she wasn't a nurse by profession, she was the best nurse I ever had. At times, she would randomly get up in the middle of the night after sleeping for a while, fix herself a weird combination of food to eat, bathe, and do dishes or wash a load of laundry. Since she was sick, I knew she wouldn't be able to do laundry or any of those other things she used to do. However, I would be there to keep her company if she were to awaken.

Unfortunately, after a few hours of staying up, my body gave me a few signals that it was time to go lie down. I started to feel ill, so I told the nurse I would go rest for a while. She told me that if anything were to happen or change with Mom, she would alert me. I wasn't going far, just to the next room. Lying there on the futon in my children's playroom, my stomach was in knots; I did my best to calm down and take deep breaths. Eventually, I fell asleep for a few hours before coming back into consciousness and realizing where I was and why. By that time, it was daylight outside with an overcast sky. The ill feeling hadn't subsided, so I tried to shake it off. I put cold water on my face, and I think I even put a cold, damp washcloth on the back of my neck to counter the nausea, but nothing seemed to work. I thought I was going to be sick, so I slipped out the front door and went outside for some fresh air. I paced down the sidewalk to the corner of our lot, trying to make myself aware of my surroundings and relax my nerves. Along the way, my mouth watered and I prayed that God would touch my body. I wanted to be there for Mom, not sick myself. I paced and spat. After a while of back and forth, up and down the sidewalk, I felt myself calming down some and finally feeling better.

I went in to check on Mom and to see if she was awake. I can't recall whether she was awake when I got in there or if she awakened after I sat next to the bed for a while. Either way, we were both glad to see each other. I leaned over the bed to kiss her and get close, and I saw her look at my hair. She reached up to touch it, said how pretty it was, and smiled until she realized her hair wasn't done. Concerned, she asked how it looked. I'm sure it was a hint for me to do something with it, but at that point, she couldn't hold her head up long enough for me to braid it. I told her it was cute, she had a ponytail at the top with some down in the back. She asked, "You sure?" Smiling, I assured her that her hair was fine. She also asked about my children; she wanted to know where they were. I felt bad because they couldn't be there, but I told her they had school, so they weren't able to make the trip this time.

There were some visitors each day who came through at various times. My aunt (one of Mom's sisters) had come into town for a few days to help my siblings with Mom's care. In addition, there was a small rotation of the caregivers in and out of the house. I sat in the lift chair and watched Mom as she tried to declare the scriptures, but her memory failed her. She looked at me, chuckled, and said, "I'm getting them all mixed up, aren't I?" I looked up some of the verses and read them to her because I hadn't been in my Word like I should have been, especially during this season. It had been quite a while since I even opened my Bible. It was encouraging to see her in such good spirits as she worshiped God in song and lifted her hands to thank and praise Him. In the middle of worship, her massage therapist walked in, set up, and began to give her a massage. The soothing smell of lavender filled the room and permeated the atmosphere alongside Mom's sweet thanksgiving to the Lord. She didn't stop or settle down, massage or not! Her masseuse joined in while massaging her arm and shoulder. As Mom thanked God, it was followed by a "Yes, He's a good God!" They joined together and welcomed His presence, it was a beautiful site to witness.

Mom was conscious for the first few days of my being there. Now and again, I would get close to her face and say, "Mom," she opened her eyes, "I love you." Her reply was, "I love you too." I held her hand, rubbed the side of her head, and soaked in all the moments, not knowing which ones would be the last. I remembered that Dad was aware for just a little while on hospice before slipping into a coma and never waking. I wondered if Mom would do the same.

She was given medicine but now in liquid form because she wasn't able to swallow pills. My sister created a chart to put on the wall to keep track of all the medications and times of scheduled administration. It got to the point where Mom eventually struggled to swallow liquids. We were told to give it to her slowly and that it would be easy for her to swallow if we gave it a certain way. However, she still choked on the medication as I stood next to the bed, her eyes wide and filled with fear as she looked at me and grabbed my hand tightly because she panicked. I tried to assure her that she was okay; but afterward, she wasn't able to take anything by mouth again.

I'm not exactly sure when it happened, but she did what I thought—she slipped into a coma. When I would go to her bedside and get real close to her, and say, "Mom," she wouldn't open her eyes. With no response, I would still say, "I love you." Each day, I would talk to her as if she were able to converse with me. I kissed her, held her hand, and swabbed her lips to keep them moisturized. At that point, I felt there was no need for the nighttime vigil nurse to continue to come to because Mom continued to lie there breathing. In my selfishness, the sound of her breathing was music to my ears–I wanted her to stay with me. A couple of months before, Mom called me and asked me to pray with her. I prayed for God to heal her and for it all to be a distant memory. When I was finished praying with her, she said (paraphrased), "I like what you said, Mese, about this all being a distant memory." At that time, I hoped that she would soon be able to tell her testimony of great healing. As I attempted to sleep in the lift recliner at night, her breathing sang a different song than one of hope. It relayed to me that it would not be long before it stopped singing altogether.

One evening, I blew up a full-sized air mattress and put it on the floor in the room with Mom. My sister, who was pregnant, my brother, and I all laid across the mattress together and listened to Mom breathe. It was a tight fit, but there was something special about the unity and staying close to her. We thought it might be her last night. I cannot recall how long we stayed there before my sister returned to her house and my brother retreated to his room, but it was time well spent–talking, lying there, just being. We all had similar thoughts and feelings.

The very next night, April 26, 2016, I turned the TV volume down low so she could listen to the gospel music channel, and I reclined in the chair next to Mom's bed. As in the past few nights, I reclined with the light of the lamp dimly illuminating the room, wondering if each night would be her last. That night felt a little different than the others, but I was so tired that I dozed off. Before I knew it, I was awakened due to hearing a change in Mom's breathing. A little startled, I remained in the fully reclined chair and watched her through the rails of the hospice bed. My heart raced as I felt like it could be her time to go, but I wouldn't move from the chair. Her chest rising and falling with each labored, rattling breath said she was close. I didn't like that song. I timed the seconds between each lyric and one of the caesuras prompted me to get up and go to her side. I longed for her to keep singing. I tenderly rubbed the side of Mom's head and tried to comfort her with my words. As she'd done so many times for me, I assured her that I was with her and that she was okay. I asked my aunt in the next room to go get my brother from downstairs. Mom took a couple more stretched-out breaths while I continued to start the stopwatch over at the end of each one to keep track. Her chest rose and dropped with each note. She breathed in and out, I restarted the stopwatch and watched each second continue to march by. I waited for her to do it again, but time just continued–tick-tock, tick-tock. I heard my brother and aunt coming down the hallway. My brother asked if she was gone. All I could do was utter how many seconds (and counting) since her last breath, even though I knew in my heart she was. I was shocked, in disbelief. I wasn't ready. I would never be ready. Regardless of everything, she'd stopped singing about 3:12 a.m., April 27, 2016 –her song was over.

Twenty-One

I now realize that business and busyness mode kicked in once Mom passed just like it did when Dad transitioned. This was a coping mechanism I didn't even know existed, let alone that I ever used it. Within moments, I thought of everything I needed to do and all the people I needed to call. I had to make sure no one told my children before I had the chance to get back home to tell and comfort them myself. God answered my prayer for me to be by Mom's side when she transitioned, so why didn't He answer the one I desperately wanted Him to, for her healing on this side?

While moving around, making calls to hospice, the funeral staff, and other necessary individuals, and answering the door for loved ones who came to be with us and see Mom one more time, it didn't occur to me to cry or be emotional. I was numb and empty, my world was at a standstill, but I knew I couldn't stop moving (especially mentally) or I just might start to feel something unwanted–pain.

When the funeral directors came for Mom, all of us who sat around her talking but mostly quiet, stepped out of the room to allow them space and time to prepare her for transport to the funeral home. We moved to the living room, still mostly quiet. It was still dark outside but my heart felt darker. Then the gurney came wheeling through the living room with Mom's body in a partially zipped body bag. A body bag–a trigger for some. Eight years before, we sat on the porch of one of my mom's best friends (they considered themselves sisters), who had passed suddenly in her sleep. As they brought her out in a body bag, Mom cried at its sight. As I sat on the sofa next to my aunt, Mom's body bag was her trigger, and she also began to cry. The sniffles rang out as some began to mourn our great loss. I went to Mom and kissed her right before she was wheeled out of the home she cultivated and dwelled in for 47 years.

The daylight hadn't shown itself yet, but it seemed like we had already been through the whole day. My sister and I left to grab food and came back. We ate but much of the day is now a blur. I remember hospice coming to pick up the bed and chair, and I also remember lying in my parent's bed on Dad's side like I'd done so many times before–my place of retreat. My sister was on Mom's side. I slept for an escape, hoping not to feel, covers on my ear and down my jawline, tucked securely under my chin. I had a slight headache and it wouldn't let up. I don't know how long we were there, but it wasn't long enough to erase the past few hours or past few months.

For the next several days, we made funeral arrangements, carefully chose Mom's final clothes, wrote her obituary, and welcomed a few visitors who came to check on us. After we took care of everything, I scheduled a flight for the evening of Sunday, May 1st. I went to church despite my feelings. While we sat in the sanctuary, service in session, I started to feel pain. Mom wasn't there sitting on her usual pew. I excused myself because there was no need for a scene, quickly walked to the restroom in the basement, and told myself that I was okay. I wiped a few tears before a close family friend, the one who used to call my dad "Unc," entered. She left her seat in the pulpit after seeing me leave out the back of the sanctuary. As my world crumbled with the realization that Mom wasn't at church, she checked on me and that made me "feel" even more. She had always been there for my family, she was one of the main voices I heard praying over me as I broke down at Dad's gravesite. That day was no different. I fought hard not to break, some tears managed to escape but I smiled and wiped them. I didn't want her to endure the weight of my pain, but I knew she would because she'd done so before. I thanked her for checking on me and we left the restroom.

That evening, my siblings and I said hard goodbyes, and I boarded my flight home. While high above the earth, I looked out at the beauty of the sun shining on the brilliantly white clouds. I wanted to capitalize on the quiet time I had, so I pulled out a small pad of paper. Once I got back home, I knew I would have to acclimate myself to being there again, just a little. I wasn't gone that long but longer than I'd ever been. During the week ahead, it may not have been as quiet as my plane time. I penned words to say about Mom for the family tribute during the funeral. I reflected on childhood memories, who Mom was, among so much more that had the potential to send me into a whirlwind of emotions. But I was taking care of business and had a deadline. I allowed myself to feel what was necessary to put a heartfelt something together that would do Mom justice but not enough to where I would go to the emotional place of no return (at least for a while). I wasn't comfortable in that place, especially around other people–too much vulnerability on display.

Once I landed later that evening, my friend picked me up from the airport so my husband could stay home with the children. Being back felt different, *life* felt different. All of my thoughts seemed to revolve around Mom's transition, missing her, or simple thoughts of her. I could tell my friend felt a little awkward and didn't know what to say once I got in her car. I'd been in that place before, so I understood. We had a normal conversation, which I appreciated in those moments because they made things feel normal for a while.

She dropped me off and I walked into a quiet home, exhausted in most ways. I felt like falling to my knees in the entryway, not to pray but to have a small meltdown. I couldn't though, too many little eyes and ears that were upstairs in bed, there was no need to startle them. My husband came to greet me and quickly returned to our room to get ready for work. I stood there in disbelief. *Did my mom not just die?* I could've opened my mouth to say I needed a hug or that I wanted to be held after all that happened and all that was witnessed. I refrained because I thought he should know I was hurting. I thought it strange that I would have to express my need for comfort. If it wasn't in his thoughts to hug me, then I didn't want it. I guess you could say some pride kicked in and rode piggyback on the wedge that had already formed between us. It didn't help that I wasn't reading my Word and as I told you before, I hadn't in quite a while. As a result, I had a minute amount of spiritual fight in me even though I had been going to church. The worst was yet to come.

I heard one of the children call out to me and I answered when suddenly, all of them came flying down the stairs. They all embraced me and it felt so good to reunite with them. They were in bed because they had school the next day, but they also knew I was coming home too–it made it hard to fall asleep. They had questions, so I told them we would go upstairs and talk about everything. Once we got into one of their rooms, I gently broke the news to them. My youngest child didn't understand what that meant. The middle two understood but not fully nor the permanence of it. My oldest completely understood and he broke down. I listened to my poor child sob and mourn his beloved MiMi. I could hear the hurt in each breath-filled cry. They were super close, so my heart ached for him.

After a long evening, everyone eventually went to sleep. My husband was at work, so I was there alone, lying still in bed with too much opportunity to feel and think. I slept to escape. The next morning, I hit the ground running. I had three days to prepare myself, my husband, and the children for the eight-and-a-half-hour road trip and once there, Mom's funeral. I dropped the oldest two off at school each day and ran many errands. I ran to a store to purchase my brother a tie that would match our color scheme, secured a rental car, got a much-needed manicure and pedicure with a dear friend, styled my oldest daughter's hair, packed many bags, shopped for road snacks and beverages, packed them, and emailed teachers in advance to see if work could be sent with my two students while they were absent from school.

After a few busy days, we left early in the morning on Thursday, May 5th. Once we arrived, we were pretty much on the go non-stop. I shared with you how Mom would wake me up on some Sunday mornings to curl her hair. I didn't mention that she also asked me to do the same thing on the morning of my wedding. I had to get over to the church to get my hair done, but of course, I took the time to get her hair together first, especially since it was a special occasion. Mom couldn't ask me to do her hair any longer, but I wanted to make sure that I styled it one last time for her, on this special occasion.

On Friday, the day before her service, I went down to the funeral home, and in the hallway right outside the morgue, I saw Mom in her casket for the first time. She was propped up, just a little so I could have better access to her hair, and she was dressed in the pretty white suit we had chosen for her. The top of her suit jacket, near her shoulders, was beautifully embroidered with a floral design and a few sequins, and it also had a pretty white satin shell under it. At first, I was a little nervous because of my surroundings and a little sad because I knew it was her final style. I would never again be able to run my fingers through her hair, create a near-perfect spiral curl, or accidentally get too close to her scalp lightly burning her with the curling iron. There was no time to be nervous or sad without getting the job done, so I talked to her and got started. "Oh, Mom." I knew she couldn't hear me, but talking to her helped me. With a comb, curling iron, and the same type of red curling wax (that I can smell as I type), I carefully took my time, used great precision, and curled each spiral in such a way to honor her. When I finished, I kept moving her curls around to make sure they were as close to perfection as I could get them. I walked away empty, knowing I would never have that privilege again.

The next morning, Saturday, May 7th, we rushed around the house getting ready. On her mother's side, Mom was the oldest of ten–seven sisters and two brothers. Six of her sisters and her two brothers were all born, raised, and lived about three hours away. We had spent time together the night before, sitting around at Mom's, talking, eating, and loving on each other. Little by little, they came into the house that morning as we planned to pray before leaving. We gathered in the front yard, bowed our heads, and prayed for God's comfort.

Mom had a nice wake and a beautiful service filled with folks from all over who came to support us and say their goodbyes. Many of them echoed the same words but in different ways over the pulpit because Mom was consistently her. My sister read the obituary and sang a song that Mom was known for singing every once in a while. After almost falling (due to a shoe malfunction) as I navigated my way behind the floral arrangements and up to the pulpit, I gave the family tribute. I witnessed my brother push through grief and operate under the power of God to give a wonderful eulogy just as he did for Dad eleven years earlier. In the end, we hugged, thanked, and shook the hands of those in attendance who came around for the final viewing. Then it was time for the three of us to close the casket. We stood there together, in the same unity Mom and Dad instilled in us, looking down at the very one who carried us until we were born, throughout our lives, and whose strength and prayers would carry us until we would meet again. Following the directions given by the funeral director, we pulled the white overlay up to Mom's neck, each of us put one hand on the lid, looked at her a final time, and in sync, closed the casket and the season of our lives of having Mom.

After her burial at the gravesite and repast, we went back to the house. I'll never forget how the house felt extra empty and the emptiness that I felt inside since her transition was amplified. I didn't know what to do with myself. My family decided to go bowling that evening, and although it was nice to spend time with everyone, I couldn't keep my mind off losing her. Every now and again, between photos with cousins and watching everyone bowl, I thought about how Mom used to bowl. I could imagine how she held the ball and everything. I knew it would take time to heal but wondered if I would ever be okay, if the things I saw and did would ever stop reflecting her, or if I would ever stop being sad.

Usually, after we got together with my out-of-town family for a funeral, wedding, or any other gathering, we made sure to have family time the next day before going our separate ways. The day after the funeral was no different as we gathered at Mom's house. She had been there all the other times, so it was a sure gut punch. It was also Mother's Day. I watched as some of my cousins celebrated their mothers and wondered if any of my aunts felt a void from losing my grandmother five years earlier. I always said that I couldn't imagine the pain of those whose mothers transitioned. The thought of losing Mom had always been unbearable, just the thought. Now, I didn't have to imagine their pain, it was with me no matter how much I tried to fight feeling it.

One of my cousins handed me a gift for Mother's Day and I thought it was the sweetest thing. I was surrounded by so much love, yet I felt hollow. I smiled for every photo we took in the front yard, enjoyed the moments with everyone, and looked on while my aunts gathered for a sister photo. My mom wasn't in it and it didn't sit well with me. I thought it was beautiful how they posed, waving toward heaven and telling Mom they missed her. We had all suffered a great loss but somehow, life had to be navigated through the aftermath.

A couple of days later, it was time for us to drive back home. My mind wouldn't settle as thoughts of leaving my brother in the house alone haunted me. He had lived there his whole life–staying after my dad died to help Mom even though she told him not to put his life on hold for her. Now, he would be by himself with thoughts of Mom amplified in the silence of the house. I wanted to make sure he was going to be okay, but I couldn't be there. So I did what I thought would help, I vacuumed and cleaned up for him. I did all I could think of that Mom usually did; I just kept moving. I know I have spoken of hard goodbyes; but the one I pushed off with cleaning that day, felt like it would send me over into that emotional place. I did not want to go there, but I could feel it surfacing. I breathed deeply through the hugs and forced my tears to dry up.

For comfort, I grabbed one of Mom's housecoats that I'd bought her several years before. The pink and white, soft fleece swallowed my hands as I held it close to my heart, and I descended the stairs of the front porch to begin life without Mom.

All the children were settling in the car when my oldest said he forgot something inside. He quickly ran inside the front door, returned a few moments later, and we backed out of the driveway. I later found out that he had gone back into the house to hug my brother again and to ask him if he was going to be okay–he even felt it. As we pulled off, my brother came outside and stood on the porch to wave goodbye. My heart broke as he stood there until he was no longer in our sight. My husband pulled onto the highway and my emotions seemed to drown me. I could no longer hold it. I took the housecoat, put it over my head, and quietly wept for what felt like hours. My head and heart ached. I couldn't call her to talk about my pain, she couldn't make it better, and because of my subtle anger, I opted not to talk to the One who could.

Twenty-Two

Life around me continued like *normal*. Life within me held on to just survive through each day. I was still wife and Mom–we needed to eat, my husband needed attention, things needed to be cleaned, laundry was like a revolving door, children needed help with homework and projects, and so on. Sleep was my refuge and it sheltered me from pain. On many days, I didn't want to get out of bed but had to because life doesn't just stop. Since I had to get up, I was determined to keep moving and stay busy. I didn't think anyone around me understood the depth of what I felt, especially my husband. He never lost anyone close to him like that, so I didn't expect him to understand. On top of that, he worked at night and slept during the day–at times, this made me feel more isolated. Still not expressing my needs due to ignorance of them and/or due to pride, more distance was created between us.

Satan capitalized on everything he could. He asked me why I prayed because God didn't hear me. If God had heard me, I would still have my parents. He told me that God was going to do what He wanted to anyway, so why even pray? I listened to him and allowed the lies to become a major part of my life. This was a huge mistake but unbeknownst to me, God would soon, thereafter, turn it around and use it.

I tried praising my way through at church but I wasn't reading my Bible nor praying at home. I didn't want to pray because it hadn't worked for me, plus I was still angry with God in a subtle way. Time passed and my wounds were not healing. As a matter of fact, I felt like they kept getting slapped because of triggers around me–I felt somewhat ignored by my husband and I'd see grandparents, parents, and children sitting down to eat at restaurants while having a great time together. The sight would make me sad and then I felt bad because I didn't think I should feel that way. Unhealthily grieving and not embracing grief led me to hold my emotions in until I couldn't. I would go into my bedroom's bathroom, shut the door, sit on the floor with my back against the door, bury my face in a towel, and scream from the build up. There was no healthy regulation of emotions, I just held them. I thought back to when Dad's cries rang out in the darkness that night. Now, I understood and felt it too. As crazy as it may sound, I tried to forget about Mom. For a while, I'd push her out of my mind every time a memory or thought surfaced. It felt like it worked, but it was just another way I unhealthily grieved.

I decided to drive all the way back home, to Mom's, with my children once school was out of session for the summer. I didn't have the support I needed to begin healing and thought once I was with my siblings, I'd feel better and get what I needed–another of Satan's tactics. My sister had just given birth to my niece and I wanted to spend time with her as well as let my sister sleep. Without knowing when we'd return, I used the process of cleaning Mom's house out to justify my month-long visit. During that month, God sent two people to me who would add to my healing. The first one was completely unexpected. He asked me how I was dealing with it. I told him I was taking it day by day but then to my surprise, he began to describe to me how I was feeling and gave details about having a spouse who couldn't relate. All I could do was listen with tears in my eyes because someone finally understood. The second person was my dear mentor and former doula. We went to lunch one day, and little did I know, it was a setup by God. Even though I didn't want to hear about prayer and reading the Word, she spoke life into me and gave me a strategy for fighting back when I was ready to do so. That day I wasn't ready and didn't know if I'd ever be.

I cleaned out Mom's closet full of suits and First Lady hats, purses, shoes, and scarves. I went through her drawers and different rooms in the house just trying to stay busy. I made myself too busy to talk to my husband when he called to check on us. I thought it was "funny" that he called to check on me when I wasn't there but while I was, he didn't check on me. I guess because he saw me functioning as usual, he assumed I was okay. It certainly was not the case, so much so, I had begun to drink alcohol to numb the pain. The wedge between us pushed us so far apart that we briefly explored divorce before he decided to get on a plane to come and salvage our marriage. It was completely salvageable but Satan didn't want that to be the case. He was also mad when my husband and I talked, put everything on the table, and worked it out.

I stayed at Mom's a couple more days after my husband returned home. I was grateful that he and I were better, but I was still hurting and I pushed my hope away because of anger. I hated the way I felt day in and day out, but it wasn't until I let go of my anger did healing begin.

After my children and I returned home, I decided that I didn't like living as I was. I told God I was going to try to pray and read again, but deep down, I didn't know if it would help me. I didn't know if He would heal my heart even though His name was (is) Jehovah-Rapha, but I had to try. I had to open my heart to Him again because He was my only hope for getting through. I had tried it my way and it proved not to work. So I applied the strategy of my mentor for two weeks. I strategically read and prayed three times per day and He met me, spoke to me, and loved on me each time. I was elated because as I kept plugging in, I gained the strength and peace I'd searched for, for months. He is always the answer.

Although still hurting, the pain could not overtake or paralyze me anymore. Grief and pain were no longer my idols. Deciding to yield my journey to Him was the best decision I could've ever made, not just for me but for generations after me and those attached to me. The road was not an easy one but God was and is completely faithful.

In 2018, God downloaded ideas for what I would later learn would be my first book. What I had gone through in the past wasn't just for me but for others also. Unsure of how it would come together, however, I knew it was to be done. At the same time, making an appointment with a therapist was a thought in my mind. Even though it had been a couple of years since Mom had passed, I felt like I needed to speak with a professional. As quickly and frequently as the idea came, it was dismissed because I thought nothing was severely wrong with me. I didn't need to relax on someone's couch and revisit my childhood or anything like that. I kept pushing it out of my mind because of false ideas and the stigmas attached. With each dismissal, God kept putting it on my heart, so I reached out to a friend to ask what I should expect from therapy. What she explained was exactly what I needed, yet I kept thinking *Do I really need to go?* Even though I felt a little off and thought talking to someone would help me, I continued to delay going.

In the late summer of 2018, my husband was presented with a better job opportunity in another state. He accepted the position and a month later, moved about four and a half hours away while the children and I stayed back so they could complete the school year. Since then, I've been asked how we navigated that time, and questions arose from others about if it was hard to go through. I must say, God knows what He's doing. That time alone allowed me to have quiet from the chaos of my busy household once I dropped my children off at school. God isolated me so that He could talk to and pour into me. I made sure to have a prayer walk most days, and I intentionally dove into my Word before starting any book writing. Those sweet, quiet times with my heavenly Daddy gave me what I needed and satisfied my soul. So even though living apart was an adjustment, I'm grateful that He had a plan for that time.

I continued the writing process, enjoying some parts of it, while other parts challenged and stretched me. The thought that my book wouldn't help anyone invaded my mind on several occasions and I almost stopped writing it, at various times. I encouraged my readers to go to therapy even though I had not done the same. God laid it on my heart again, much heavier. At my church's New Year's Eve service, my pastor said something that confirmed it was time for me to find a therapist. Within the next day or so, I found one. After the initial consultation, it was time to get started.

My first session benefitted me to the point where I felt different and quickly realized that I should've gone a long time ago. After those 50 minutes, I felt empowered and encouraged in the Lord; my perspective on life had shifted a little. God spoke to me through my therapist and I knew I had made the right decision. Over the years, there had been so many life changes and hurdles to jump over (add a second upcoming relocation), but I'd never taken the time to properly process it all. Instead, I kept going, getting further pushed behind the scenes of being a wife, a mom, and everything else I was to everyone else. Somehow, I had forgotten to take care of myself. I'd gotten away from who God intended me to be. I began to identify with someone I wasn't, and it felt normal. There was a push to find me again. I was still in the process of healing. Therapy allowed me to deal with the hurt head-on and get to the other side of it. I was close to healing and getting off the rollercoaster of grief, according to my therapist, so I knew God started it and He would complete it. (Insert victory run here.)

I had a session every week for the following four months. During that time, there were many revelations from God–I realized He gave my parents the ultimate healing. Had He done it on earth like I wanted, it would've been temporary. He showed me a great deal about myself and so much more. I could go into more detail here, but I'd rather you go to see for yourself (smile). One of the most important things that happened in therapy, though, was God revealing to me how I was to execute my purpose on earth. Once He showed it to me and confirmed it through my therapist, I had a vision for my life. My obedience to go to therapy, as God instructed, landed me in a place to receive what He had for me. He did more for me than I would have ever expected. Needless to say, I walked away from therapy with a renewed sense of self–stronger, happier, healthier, and whole. I desired for everyone to have the same type of experience, and I was passionate about helping them reach their purpose.

Before moving, I dedicated my time to becoming a certified life coach. I found that the coursework excited me, so I looked forward to it. It didn't quite feel like work but rather an extension of who I was and what I did naturally. With my certification, I honed my God-given skills to better help people thrive through difficult times in life, set and reach goals, and walk in their God-given purpose.

During that time, the more I sought God, the more He gave me direction and clarity on the next steps. I was humbled by how He worked in my life. He planted a vision inside me that I didn't think I could carry out, but He knew that I could because I would stay close to Him. After nine months (the number nine in scripture represents completeness or finality; the end of one cycle and the beginning of another), not only was the book birthed, but our family was reunited as my children and I moved to be with my husband.

Starting over in a new state for the second time wasn't as difficult as it was the first time. Within two months of moving, God put me in a community of women that I wasn't looking for but absolutely needed. Through these amazing women, God has provided support, friends, prayer partners, and spiritual guidance. We take deep dives into the Word together, learn from, and encourage one another. This community has been a life-changer because it has taken my faith to another level. By consistently studying the Word on my own and with others, I have come to know God better and gained a deeper understanding of His character. He has progressively revealed more and more of Himself to me, not just as God but as my Father.

Twenty-Three

Not long after the move, one of my best friends and I had a conversation in which she asked me how I viewed my father. Of course, I viewed him as a wonderful, loving father, but with more exploration, I realized I also viewed him as an authoritarian. This wasn't a bad thing, nor did it reflect negatively, but it did influence the limitations I put on my view of God.

My father, an ex-marine, was a loving person and in love, he was a disciplinarian and more strict than my mother who was a laid-back nurturer. His role as bishop was also a filter through which I saw him. Some of the decisions he made for our family were based on who he was called to be and his responsibilities in that call. For these reasons and more, his authoritative side rang out louder to me than the intimate side. He would always tell me that I could talk to him about any and everything, and I knew I could. While he would reiterate that fact every now and then, the thoughts in my head were that I would not bring everything to him because of my fears and views of him. There were limitations to how I approached him and with what I approached him just because of how I saw him.

There was a conversation that he and I had that started pretty casually but quickly became serious. I think I was in my late teens when somehow it came out that I had always been a little afraid of him. Shocking to me, he was pretty surprised to hear it. I gave him a few examples and Dad felt bad. He expressed how he never wanted any of us to be afraid of him and I could see that it didn't sit well with him. For a while, I tried to justify my fear as a healthy reverent one, and it may have been to an extent. However, it did keep me from experiencing the fullness of Dad.

Both our earthly fathers and heavenly Father hold positions of authority in our lives. Our earthly fathers are responsible for our upbringing, discipline, and guidance during our childhood and teenage years. Our heavenly Father, on the other hand, is the ultimate authority in our lives as He created us, sustains us, and governs our future outcomes and the universe.

Both fathers, earthly and heavenly, have the capacity to love their children unconditionally. Our earthly fathers may not always express their love in the way we want or expect, but their love for us is often selfless and enduring, in some cases. Similarly, our heavenly Father's love for us is perfect, unchanging, and unconditional, no matter what we do or fail to do. While our earthly fathers are capable of great love and wisdom, they are also human and therefore, fallible. They may make mistakes, have personal shortcomings, and even fail us at times. In contrast, our heavenly Father is perfect and never makes a mistake or fails us. His wisdom and love are infinite and flawless.

God opened my eyes to see that I wasn't really viewing Him as my Father (relationally) but mostly as God (authoritatively), just like I viewed my earthly father. For years, I limited myself from experiencing His fullness. He was (is) both God and my Father. The more I understood that, the more He called me to intimacy with Him–I talked to Him more, cried before Him a lot more, and my desire to spend time with Him increased.

Our relationships with our fathers, negative, positive, non-existent, healthy, estranged, or whatever the case may be, have a great influence on our relationship with our heavenly Father. If the earthly relationship was (is) negative, in any way, it can put a cap on how you will trust God or if you will trust Him fully. The negativity often causes us to put God in a box that we are comfortable with, but it also stops us from experiencing Him in His fullness. If the experience was (is) positive, there may still be a box you put God in because earthly fathers are limited. God has no limits.

Satan wants our view of our heavenly Father to be misconstrued. The misconception may start as early as childhood and stick with us into adulthood. He will not only use our relationship with our earthly fathers but also any relationships we have. In some of our earthly relationships, we have been abused (abnormal use) by other humans. Often, we don't even realize it. Satan is well aware and hopes to keep us from seeing God clearly. He knows that in God's presence is the fullness of joy, but He doesn't want you to experience it.

Since our relationship with our heavenly Father is the most powerful influence in our lives, shaping our attitudes, behaviors, and beliefs towards ourselves and others, Satan wants to blur the lines. Because our relationship with God transforms us from the inside out and equips us to live a life that honors Him and blesses those around us, it pushes us toward purpose. If we realize our purpose and have a vision for our lives, then Satan's influence is greatly diminished.

I challenge you to give some thought to how your relationships have influenced the most important relationship in your life (the one with God). More importantly, I challenge you to allow your relationship with Him to be the one that influences all the others (the secondary ones). There is a call from the Lord to go deeper in Him–deeper in knowledge, deeper relationally, and deeper in intimacy.

Whatever the situation was (is) with your father, God fills every void and has divine connections set up to meet your needs. When you join the body of Christ, your spiritual family can provide what your physical family has not. We have a Daddy in Him–the perfect one who will be with us always. Our earthly fathers have a limited time with us, as they age and eventually pass away. Our relationship with our heavenly Father, however, is eternal. He offers us the promise of eternal life through faith in Jesus Christ, and our relationship with Him will continue beyond this life into eternity. If your earthly daddy (parents) never pointed you toward your heavenly Daddy, this book is your call to greater intimacy with Him. God is our Everlasting Father.

As you've read, I struggled after both of my parents' transitions. Of course, I grieved, especially after my mom left, and I did an internal plummet. I was not depending on God to see me through or to be with me during that time. Naturally, I was dependent on my parents for much. After my break up with Jon, I referenced my motto in a conversation with Dad: People come and people go. At that time, I never considered that ALL people come and go, and I've often said, "Family is forever," not in the literal sense. In the midst of writing, God spoke these words to my heart: "I am the only One who never comes and goes."

My Father is not seasonal. Everything and every person in my life (or I in theirs) has or will become seasonal except Him. Mom and Dad came and went, they weren't mine, to begin with. They were always His, loaned to me as the conduit to get me to the earth.

My foundation wasn't ultimately in my parents or anyone else but in God alone. God called me to come forth through them, and He called them to raise me in fear and admonition of Him. They were to point me in His direction so He could mold me to fulfill the purposes He has for me here. They set me up for life without them on earth. Eventually, I was able to grab a hold of that and depend on my heavenly Father to be what He already was. I took the limits off.

This perspective challenged me but also helped me greatly as I became more dependent on Him. I could no longer depend on my parents, but I had other family and friends I relied on. So God started shifting people in my life to get me to look to Him first. I was one to seek comfort through food, entertainment, or talking on the phone rather than finding it in the Comforter. He had to strip me of some dependencies that I didn't know were hindering me in my relationship with Him.

Dependence on the Holy Spirit will always trump dependence on people or anything else. The Holy Spirit will link you with the right people through whom He will bless you. When I realized people couldn't do what God could do for me, it helped me stay closer to Him than anyone else. Staying close to Him has opened the door for continual healing from the cares of this life and continuously renews my mind to be successful in progressing through all He has for me.

Before concluding this book, I'd like to tell you the rest of the wood-in-my-foot story. As I stated, I could tell something still wasn't right with my foot. It was uncomfortable to walk or put pressure on it but it wasn't just sore, it hurt. I thought I would feel better after sleeping for the night, but when I woke up to get ready for church the next morning, my foot seemed to hurt worse. I hobbled to the breakfast table, spilling orange juice out of my cup on the way. Dad sort of scolded me because I guess he thought I was playing or being dramatic.

By the time we got to church, I couldn't walk in, so my brother carried me into the sanctuary and it was quite embarrassing. Sunday school hadn't started; so before it did, Mom had my brother carry me out into a room connected to the vestibule. As I sat on the sofa, Mom asked me a few questions, and she may have examined my foot. Nothing appeared wrong other than the wound. She sent word to my dad that she and my sister were going to take me to Children's Hospital.

I was nervous because I didn't want any shots or anything like that. In my young mind, I didn't know what would happen. They gave me an X-ray which showed that there was still wood in my foot that wasn't visible on the surface. I would have to go through minor surgery for them to retrieve it. *Surgery?* I'd never undergone surgery before. Mom called over to the church to let Dad know and he, of course, felt bad for scolding me and thinking I was acting. He asked Mom to put me on the phone and he apologized to me.

I didn't get put to sleep but had to receive numbing shots for a local anesthetic. While positioned on the table, tears rolled out of the corners of my eyes because it hurt–but mostly due to fear. I kept wanting to know if I was bleeding a lot, I was just rattled. After everything was cleaned up and my foot all better, they put the long (almost the length of a toothpick) chunk of wood in a sealed tube for me to take. I couldn't believe they pulled that from my foot, but I was glad it was over.

I knew I wasn't crazy or making the pain up. Something still felt wrong after the problem was taken care of at the surface. I thought to myself that if my friend's mother had just left my foot alone and taken me to my daddy as I asked, I might not have had to have surgery. She snatched the wood out and left residue behind. I'd like to think my dad would have been more precise and removed it all rather than perform a quick fix and not check for other damage.

When God handles it, no residue will be left behind. When He fixes your pain, He heals you of that thing completely. There may be a process involved, but ultimately He will heal you. Other people cannot fix what only God can. Going to people, alcohol, food, and entertainment for relief is a surface thing. God is the only one who can heal the root.

Even though the storms of life will continue to come, He's given me the grace to dance in the rain. I can relax knowing that He is with me through the howl of the strong winds, the piercing lightning, and the uncertainty of direction. Even though each storm has its own duration, I can always look back at how He's taken me through before. With that in mind, I can encourage myself that He will do it again.

Storms aren't always easy and often bring anxiety, worry, or fear. At His feet is where I can fall apart and release every emotion. He tells me to cast my cares on Him because He cares for me. He is my security and my safe place. He is the One who takes every one of my tears and understands what each means. He is the One who heals every one of my hurts. In all of my achievements, He is the One who causes me to succeed. He is the One who loved me first and loves me best. In Him, I have found a perfect love that's the foundation of my life. I've been captured by it and have never been more free.

As many times as I have fallen and as much as I felt like I have failed God, He's never loved me any less or changed His mind about me. With every tear I cry or problem I face (whether self-inflicted or otherwise), He's always there, even when I don't turn my eyes to Him. He patiently and relentlessly pursues me. He lovingly embraces and overwhelms me with His presence to remind me that He's with me–it's always been and will always be Him. As my life's story unfolds, I hold onto the truth that my identity is rooted in God alone. Looking back through the pages of my life, I see how it's been intricately woven together by nothing other than the hand of God. He has used every storm and experience to draw me closer to Himself. I'll keep looking to Him for guidance, comfort, and strength, knowing that I am forever His beloved daughter.

Acknowledgments

First and foremost, I thank God, my heavenly Daddy. As stated in the title, it's always been Him. Father, thank You for revealing Yourself to me each day. Thank you for my life. Thank you for the realization that apart from You, I can do nothing and I am nothing. Thank you for being my stability, my safe place, and my light. In you I find everything I need and everything I need is found in You. Thank you for sitting with me and allowing me to partner with you to complete this book. Thank you that this book is a seed for someone. I didn't think I could write it or that I would ever finish it. I was correct, I could not, not without You. So, thank you again. Thank You for shining on me, so that I can reflect You. I love You, and I praise You.

Even though you both are no longer here with me, I honor you and thank you for the lives you lived inside and outside our home. Thank you for being consistently you. Thank you for living lives that spoke for themselves. Thank you for setting me up for life without you. Even though you are missed tremendously, I am happy for you both. I would hope that if you could see me today, you would be proud. I love you Mom and Dad.

You see me and love me in the good and bad times. You're patient with me through it all. Thank you for loving me for who I am and for being consitent in your pursuit of me. Thank you for supporting me in my endeavors. I know the process of this book has not only been felt by me, but it's also been felt by you. Thank you for those days you told me, "Go write; I've got them." Thank you for believing in me. Even though I know you may have thought I was a little crazy when you'd wake up to lights and me on my computer in the middle of the night, but thank you for bearing with me. It's all done now, and it's a little unbelievable. You listened to my ideas and let me read to you. I appreciate and love you, Husband.

To my precious children. I thank each of you for your support, love, and patience. I know this book has pulled me away some, but you all have loved me through it and allowed me the time I needed to finish. Even though much of the time was interrupted, you all always came back to shut my door when I asked you to, smile! You all are my joy. You each have taught me so much about myself, about life, and about love. I thank God for allowing me to be your mother; it's such a privilege to raise you and have you in my life. I pray that my life displays God's love to you. Also, I pray that you know and remember that inside you is everything you need to do (and be) what God's called you to. You are my gift, you have great purpose, and I love you.

Thank you to my siblings for walking this journey with me. I know I've called you both several times to reminisce and recall memories, so thank you for going down memory lane with me. Thank you for being the best siblings and for continuing to stay close with me, how we've always been. It will never change. I know some siblings fight and don't talk for months or years, but I can't imagine that. I'm glad that's never been and will never be us. I love you both.

To Dr. Marianne Edwards. Thank you so much for your help. I appreciate you greatly. With everything you had going on in your own life, you were determined to show your love for me through your help. I don't take it for granted. I appreciate the love and support. I love you.

To Dr. Matisa Wilbon. Thank you for taking time out of your full schedule to write the foreword for this book. I appreciate your support down through the years, your friendship, and your love. I'm so proud of you. Thank you for being a great example to me. I love you.

Thank you to my friends and family who have listened to me talk about this book for what seems to be years now. There are just a few of you who knew about it, but thank you for keeping up with me and encouraging me through the process. You know who you are. A special thank you to my cousin, Amanee, who spent much time with me drafting book covers, only for me to not go with any of the drafts we created. Thank you for your patience and skills, cousin. I love you and ya'll.

To you, the reader. Thank you so much for purchasing this book, and for walking through my journey. I pray that in some great way, you've met with God, received healing, laughed, or maybe even shed cleansing tears. I pray that your eyes have been opened to something new about you and/or about God. I'm excited for your life's journey and for what this book has stirred in you. I may or may not know you personally or well, but I love you. Thanks for reading.

Connect with the Author

Hi there,

Thank you for your purchase of my book. I hope you've enjoyed it. I welcome your feedback and review on Amazon and on my website (listed below).

I would love for us to stay connected. You can do this by following me on these social media platforms:

Facebook, Instagram, and YouTube: @yourbestdash

Also, don't forget to grab your copies of my other book and study guide, *Are You Living YOUR Best Dash?* and your apparel on my website:

www.yourbestdash.com

Lastly, you can email me at yourbestdash@gmail.com.

I look forward to hearing from you soon.

Mariesa ♥